6 FIGURES AND BEYOND

Creating **Success** in Network Marketing

Rob Sperry | Amanda Simon | Andrew Logan | Angie Gischel
Ariella Hendershaw | Ashley Stanley | Beth Graves
Jackie Wilson | Joanna Bacon | Jen McCann
Jennifer Stroman | Jill & Gabe Pearson | Jordan LeVeck
Kelli Jochum | Lori Hayes | Lynn Cooper | Miss Marilyn
Megan Bond | Melissa Hartmann | Nina Salkic
Shylo Bijold | Sue Brenchley | Toccara Johnson | Tyronica Carter

TGON Publishing

© 2021 TGON Publishing. All Rights Reserved

Reproduction or translation of any part of this book beyond that permitted by Section 107 or 108 of the 1976 United States Copyright Act without written permission of the copyright owner is unlawful. Criminal copyright infringement is investigated by the FBI and may constitute a felony with a maximum penalty of up to five years in prison and/or a $250,000 fine. Request for permission or further information should be addressed to TGON Publishing.

Warning—Disclaimer

The purpose of this book is to educate and inspire. This book is not intended to give advice or make promises or guarantees that anyone following the ideas, tips, suggestions, techniques or strategies will have the same results as the people listed throughout the stories contained herein. The author, publisher and distributor(s) shall have neither liability nor responsibility to anyone with respect to any loss or damage caused, or alleged to be caused, directly or indirectly by the information contained in this book.

ISBN: 978-1-7358447-3-2

CONTENTS

INTRODUCTION

"Alone, we can do so little. Together we can do so much."

– Helen Keller

I remember going to one of my first general network events. I was excited to meet new people, to network with others, and get inspired by what was being accomplished in the industry. For the most part, everyone was terrific, and it was everything that I thought it would be until I met *That Guy*. You know the one - the cocky guy who touts himself as *everything* and shares nothing. The guy that puts down others to validate that he is better than everyone else. The loudest guy in the room, yet he is saying nothing – or nothing of value, at least. Yep, there he was, doing all those things loudly for everyone to hear.

I believe that there are lessons to learn from everyone. As I sat and listened to *That Guy* talk on and on about how great he was and how terrible the rest of us were, a lesson popped into my head. I knew what I wanted to learn from him. *That Guy* was showing me the type of leader I never wanted to be. I realized I never wanted to talk badly about other companies. I never wanted people to walk away from me feeling bad about themselves. I would always collaborate and would always add value, regardless of what company someone was from. I would always listen to others and let them know how much I valued them. I would be a source for good and an example of why everyone wants to be a part of network marketing.

At that instant, a huge smile spread across my face, and *That Guy* said, "Why are you smiling? Unless you have my paycheck, you shouldn't be smiling at anything." I told him I had learned a lot from listening, and then thanked him for his time and walked away.

Throughout all my years in network marketing, and now as a coach for people in the industry, I invest a lot of my energy, money, and ideas in developing ways to network, collaborate, and build others wherever they are. I love to over-deliver value!

I do this by hosting online virtual retreats, having in-person breakthrough retreats, and hosting some of the most successful six and seven-figure masterminds in the network marketing industry. Another thing that I do is give brilliant, successful people a chance to share their wealth of knowledge by having them co-write books with me.

Of course, I have my own stories, experiences, and knowledge about the industry to share. But it pales in comparison to what can be shared when I bring the brightest and best into a book with me. These authors bring new insights that I haven't had. They bring life experiences that I have never had, either. And they create a connection with you that is unique and different from my own. This collaboration means you get the best possible value out of reading my books.

Bill Nye, aka "The Science Guy," said, "Everyone you meet knows something you don't." Bill Nye wasn't famous for inventing anything or finding any new species. Instead, he got famous by collaborating, sharing, and networking with others. I believe there is so much value in collaborating and networking, and Bill Nye proves that. The very first book I ever wrote, *The Game of Networking*, is all about this topic. My passion for sharing and collaborating inspired me to create a series of books with other authors in the network marketing industry. These books serve as sources of knowledge, experience, and connection.

I have hand-selected top names in the industry to collaborate on the book you are reading or listening to right now. The authors in this book will share actionable steps that you can take in your business today that could ultimately lead to your success. For example, one of the authors in this book told me, "I was close to the top rank in the company but felt completely stuck. Nothing my sponsor said helped. It wasn't until I read your very first collaboration book that my huge breakthrough came." She implemented what she learned from that book, and success quickly followed.

This book is here to help you achieve six figures and beyond. As I read through the book, I was taking notes! There are some valuable lessons and tools that you can use starting today. But you have to be willing to commit and take action. Six-figure businesses don't happen by themselves. It takes people like you who are eager to get to work and keep working until it happens. We know you can do it, and we want to help you do it – that's a powerful combination. You won't find *That Guy* among any of these authors. All you will find are fantastic minds ready to share their secrets to help you have your next breakthrough success.

If you're anything like me, you should get a pen and paper ready because you will want to take notes.

AMANDA SIMON

Achievements:

- She reached the top 0.25% earners in a company in 18 months while working full time as a teacher
- $10 million teams of 2,000 within four years of being in network marketing
- Achiever of every company incentive/promotion/challenge, including top ten enrollers for three consecutive years
- Two-time trainer at National Conference, Leadership Summit, company calls
- Former two-sport Division I athlete, boy-mom, tomboy who made it with a beauty brand
- Married 28 years, she splits her time between her Florida home, Alabama lake house, and Adirondack cabin

Quote:

"If you don't have something nice to say,
***find* something nice to say."**

Coach's Notes:

I have personally coached Amanda for the last nine months. To give you a little background, she successfully built a massive organization while being a full-time teacher. This is important to point out because many think that you need to throw yourself into network marketing full time to have success. Amanda proved that wrong.

She achieved such success because she has an immense focus on the essential principles of network marketing. Her teaching background helps her to simplify complex information to give you the meat of any training. Pay close attention!

Edification makes people want to work with you.

Put simply, my job is to help people get what they want. That is the job of any network marketing leader. We are in this field because of our desire to serve others. We can provide access to products, services, and the potential creation of one's own business and income.

My number one priority in network marketing has always been helping my team grow. I do this by making myself available to share what I have learned and done. This approach ensures every person on my team has the same opportunity to get what they want from their network marketing business as I have.

Every good leader in our field recognizes that we work for our downline; our downline does not work for us. I realized this early on in my career when the importance of edification became apparent. I can do my job much more easily when my team is edifying me. Much the same, my team grows exponentially when I become better at edifying them. Edification is a skill that every single leader needs to recognize, learn, master, and teach.

I credit my success in network marketing to the fact that I have been a student of great thinkers and successful network marketers over time. When I enrolled with my company, I realized that to be successful; I had to learn to think like successful people do. As a result, I have spent the last four years with my nose buried in books.

I can generally put my books into two piles. I can stack books on positive mental attitude and the **mindset** necessary to achieve greatness and success in the first pile. Secondly, I can stack more technical books, written by network marketing professionals, containing industry-specific information to help me develop the necessary **skillset** for success in the industry. I have read hundreds of books on mindset and skillsets. Yet, in all the books that I have read, I only saw any mention of edification once.

Because I have seen firsthand what a crucial component edification can be in growing a large and successful organization, I realized it was the perfect topic to cover in this collaborative effort. This chapter will share the who, what, how, when, and why of edification. Appropriately used, modeled regularly, and taught explicitly, this skill will positively impact your team's belief, culture, growth, and success.

Whether you notice it or not, edification is happening all around you all the time. It occurs when a person introduces someone and tells you about some of their accomplishments. It happens when we hear some fantastic speakers presented on stage. It even happens when we are making recommendations to our friends of the best places to do business.

When we listen to an introduction of someone who is about to speak on stage, it creates excitement. We want to hear more. We generally learn of the speaker's accomplishments and achievements. It makes us feel fortunate to have the opportunity to learn from that speaker. When we have heard someone properly edified, we are more willing and excited to listen and follow the advice they have for us - this is an obvious example of edification. If no introduction is given and a person merely saunters onto the stage, grabs a mic, and begins rambling, we would be less likely to accept what they say and more likely to question the validity of their information. The fact that the person speaking has achieved a certain level of success, and we know it, provides credibility. Edification is the *intentional* telling of someone's success to someone else to get people to know, like, and trust that person as well as those associated with that person. So, sit back, open your mind, and let me share a critical piece of what I've learned; what edification has to do with network marketing and why it is an essential component in building a thriving network marketing business.

The concept of edification is vital to identify, learn, practice, and teach. Early on in my network marketing journey, I had a situation with my upline lady, who was not familiar with the concept of edification. I naturally edified her when she started coming in to work locally with my team. I edified her before our first meeting, getting my team excited and promoting the event.

I spoke of her accomplishments and achievements and consistently reminded my team that if I wanted to achieve what she had achieved, I had to learn to think as she thought. The only way that was going to happen was to spend time with her. So, I promoted that meeting to everyone in my downline. Of course, the most significant promoters have the most prominent teams and tremendous success, but that's another chapter.

I will never forget that first meeting. She was standing in front of the room waiting for her introduction. I started mentioning her accomplishments and success while speaking of the valuable lessons learned from her. I could see she was visibly uncomfortable standing before the crowd while I continued to talk of her success. I know she wanted to crawl under the table, but that didn't stop me.

We discussed it afterward, and I explained the respect I have for what she has accomplished. I wanted my team to recognize the value of her time and experience and know how lucky we were that she came in to work with us. As my team watched me edify her, they began to do the same thing. Our numbers were small initially, but I would continue to edify her each time she returned to my area.

I would have my team and my potential teammates excited to meet her. My team learned to do the same. We more than tripled our attendance numbers at those meetings in about six months. My team was growing and on fire; we were creating and promoting leaders, and my upline quickly understood the power of edification. She then began to edify my leaders and me, and now it has become something that our team is doing very effectively, upline, downline, and crossline.

Coach's Notes:

With social media advances, people have forgotten many of the timeless marketing principles. Don't get me wrong, social media is a huge benefit, but there are some weaknesses with it. For example, many have forgotten the basics of edification. Edifying is one of the timeless principles that will help your business tremendously, but it is rarely taught. As I already mentioned, much of Amanda's success has come from sticking to timeless principles. She has broken down the power of edification. Now she will go even deeper on the finer intricacies for you to master the edification process truly.

Who, What, When, Why, and How

What is edification? Edification is when you help another person achieve credibility. To edify is to build up and speak highly of another person and make them experts on a particular subject. Network marketing usually involves talking with prospects or your downline about your upline's success and accomplishments with your company, even before they have met them.

Who do we edify? We edify everyone as often as we can. Everyone loves a positive person and loves to meet positive people. We can edify our upline leaders, downline, crossline cousins, home office staff, and other successful network marketers and leaders.

Why do we edify? Edifying your upline will give it as much influence as possible with the people you introduce to them. It will position your upline "experts," which will increase the likelihood that somebody will listen to what they have to say. If it is done correctly, edification will give your prospect/potential teammate the feeling that s/he is very fortunate to have the opportunity to speak with your upline. Finally, it provides your upline "celebrity status." This status makes your upline's job of helping you grow your team that much easier.

When do we edify? *All the time*! Yep, all the time - to our existing team and our prospects.

That said, here are some specific times where edification can be highly effective:

Third-party calls

Perhaps your upline offers you the chance to do three-way calls. As you are in the process of sharing your business opportunity, you want to be sharing some of your team's success and your upline's expertise and accomplishments. You want to make your upline an authority. When you have your prospect on a call with your upline, that prospect will be more likely to listen to the message your upline is delivering.

Local meet-ups, team socials, training

Edify your upline leader to anyone in your downline for any type of team connections. You want your team excited to have the opportunity to spend time with someone successful and knowledgeable. You want your downline to listen, learn and ask questions of your upline, and you want your downline to respect what your upline has achieved and feel fortunate to have the chance to learn from them.

Team opportunity calls

If your team hosts opportunity calls where you can invite your prospects to learn more about your company, edify whoever is giving the presentation. You should be building up that presenter and making that prospect feel fortunate even to have the opportunity to listen to what your upline or the presenter has to say. If *you* are the presenter, be sure to edify your leaders and credit your success to the quality people surrounding you.

In-person opportunity meetings

You can edify your upline or the presenter at an upcoming opportunity meeting. You can let that prospect know that s/he will have the chance to meet a very successful leader with your company. Assure your prospect that your upline will be excited to meet them. Be sure to make that introduction at some point before or after the meeting.

National conference or annual convention

It is essential to edify your upline and other company leaders who get your team to the conference. Assure them that they will have a chance to meet and learn from some of the company's most notable leaders. Side note: National Conference changes lives. After attending my first one, I left, was promoted three times in six months to the executive level and walked the stage at the following year's conference for the first time as a top ten enroller. The best advice here is to edify your leaders and get your people to conferences! The conference builds belief, belief creates activity, and activity brings results.

Company-sponsored incentive trips

If your company hosts any incentive trips that your team can earn, edifying your upline and other company leaders will have them excited about achieving an invitation. If done correctly, one of the biggest reasons that somebody will want to earn those trips is because they get to rub elbows with the "celebrities" of your company. Leaders get that celebrity status because we give it to each other when we properly edify.

Most often, what people really want to know is the *how*. How do I edify someone else? How am I supposed to know what to say? First, ask the person you are introducing what s/he would like you to say! It is that simple. If you are getting up in front of a room to present your upline, you can ask your upline, "Is there anything, in particular, you would like me to highlight as I introduce you?" It's that easy.

Another great way is to look at their social media accounts or websites. Their profile or "about" section is a resource you can use when looking for key points to mention during an introduction. You must also remember why this group of people is gathering and why this person will be vital to them and their success. If you are in a room full of teachers, and your upline is a former elementary teacher, include that! Build that *know*, *like*, and *trust* factor any time you can.

Keep it sweet, simple, honest, sincere, and authentic.

An easy way to do it:

- Offer your upline's background
- Offer a point or two about their current position
- Include information about their future plans

As you are edifying, these are things you should touch on:

- Money/success – top income earner/successful
- Facts – she knows what she is doing, proven success
- Fun – we have a blast together, take trips, enjoy our friendship
- Help – continues to teach and train and mentor others; we're part of a winning team

For those of you still stuck on the *how, here* is an example of a good, edifying introduction.

Janet is my upline, and I am introducing her to a room full of professional working moms at a network marketing event. Notice in the introduction below, I have touched on the components listed above. Can you find each one?

"I am so excited that you have the chance to meet Janet. She is a mom of four and a former engineer. She is one of our company's first stylists with one of the company's largest and most successful teams. Janet knows what she's doing and how to build success. We have a blast working together and traveling, and I just love that she's my teacher and my mentor. What's really cool is that Janet has also become my friend. She has taught me a lot about building a successful team and is the reason I have achieved what I have. My team and I love learning from her and taking advantage of her expertise. As successful as she is, she is committed to continuing to mentor others. I can't wait for you to have the chance to meet her. You are going to love her!"

Leaders need to edify too

Up until this point, most of what has been covered has discussed the downline's need to edify the upline. Leaders, now let's talk about you. Edification is for you, too, with every single member of your team. If you are a leader, it is critical to edify your downlines. Speak of your downline in front of them as if they are already where you want them to be. They will become what you believe they will become. If they hear you say it and know that you believe in them, they will become successful. Your belief in them needs to be there, even when theirs is not.

When I am doing a three-way call for my downline, edification will happen for all three parties. On that call, I will tell that prospect how lucky she is to know whoever invited her – of course, that is my downline. I will say positive things about my teammate, even if she is brand new.

I can speak of her excitement and her energy. I can talk about her eagerness to learn and say that I see she has what it takes, and I can't wait to watch her grow. Obviously, if the teammate is already an established leader, I can say that she is one of my best leaders and that the prospect can learn so much from her. I can also say that I am so lucky I can work with her and learn from her myself. My downline will edify me, sharing some of our team's success and achievements. She will also edify the prospect when she introduces him/her to me while specifically explaining why she thinks the prospect will be great at what we are doing.

Leaders, remember, *nothing* negative ever goes downline or to a prospect, even if you have an issue, problem, or concern with your upline or company. Negativity will slowly erode your business if you send it downline. Your downline will also duplicate it, and people will say negative things about you. As leaders grow, their downlines will look to criticize instead of spreading value and respect, creating a toxic environment on your team. Instead, lift and inspire everyone!

Always address concerns with your upline, but do not ever speak negatively about your company or upline with your team. If your downline comes to you with a problem or complaint, listen and validate, but don't bash your company or upline. Always, always, always, always edify and be positive. Respect what your leaders have accomplished. Realize you will be where they are when you do what they have done. Duplicate their effort, and you will duplicate their success. There is no need to do it "better" if the results support that that is a simple way to do it that can be easily duplicated. Network marketing is *not* about what you can do - it is about what you can duplicate. Edification is a simple process to identify, learn, model, and duplicate.

You have probably heard the saying, "If you don't have something nice to say, don't say anything at all." Well, that was never good enough in the Simon family, especially raising three boys who could be cranky during those teenage years. So, we modified that phrase to, "If you don't have something nice to say, *find* something nice to say." I guarantee that you can find something nice to say about everybody if you try. If you edify your upline, you edify your downline, and master this critical network marketing skill; your team will duplicate it. By duplicating this, you will create a culture that is uplifting and positive. People will want to become a part of this community, and you will grow an enormous, profitable, and fun business. I encourage you to work on the application of this skill and teach it to your team. It will revolutionize your business and accelerate your growth.

Coach's Notes:

One thing Amanda said that stood out from this last section was this: "Your belief in them needs to be there, even when theirs is not." When I first started, my mentor would constantly pull me aside and tell me that I would be one of the best in the network marketing industry one day. He told me to work hard, work smart, be humble, and always be willing to learn. Eventually, he told me that I was already one of the best. He taught me not to base my confidence on my paycheck but to keep at it. His words were so empowering. He believed in me more than I believed in myself. This gave me the confidence to keep pushing on during those down moments. Believe in others and see the best in them. Tell them what you see!

ANDREW LOGAN

Achievements:

- Joined the network marketing industry just before turning thirty - purely as a product customer

- He started building a business with his wife Angie once she became pregnant - wanting a different life for their family moving forward

- He now leads a team of almost 100,000 people, is a Top 5 income earner in their company in Australia, and has earned multiple seven figures over the past nine years

- He has leveraged his network marketing success into a property investment portfolio consisting of 16 houses

Quote:

"Wealth is the Ability to Fully Experience Life."

- Henry David Thoreau

Financial Freedom is possible

I am passionate about helping people achieve financial freedom through the network marketing industry. The potential for financial freedom is one of the main reasons people join our industry. But unfortunately, many people will struggle to reach their goals. And worse - often it's because we don't provide the correct tools to help people achieve true wealth and freedom. As an industry, we are great at helping people earn more money. Giving them systems, tools, and scripts to launch their business and bring in an extra income. But there's a difference between earning money and having freedom. Network marketing is the very best way to start on the path to financial freedom - but it's only one half of the picture. The other half is helping people manage and multiply their money. Nobody ever found freedom from spending all their money straight away. As an industry we can struggle there. Which is a shame; because we have the best kept secret in financial freedom - as long as we show people how to turn their extra money into wealth.

The word 'freedom' conjures up a lot of great vision and excitement. It can create visceral feelings in your stomach that speak to possibilities and dreams. But we also need to match our vision and dreams with a step by step process. In this chapter, I want to share with you the road map to financial freedom. Take you through the four stages through which we progress; help you work out where you are and how to get to the next stage. If you follow these steps, in order, you can go from zero to financially free. You will be able to achieve all the dreams on your vision board, live your dream day every day.

If you were to rewind and see me in high school, you would see a kid focused on getting good grades. Good grades meant that I could get into a good college, which would help me get a good job. So I went to university, got my undergrad in medicine, and followed the expected path to become a physical therapist.

I thought at the time that getting into the medical industry meant I would get paid well and be able to travel - working with athletes and teams all around the world. As an 18 year old, at the time, that would mean freedom.

Looking back - I was in stage one of financial freedom. Stage one is being an employee. In stage one, we are trading time for money. Learning skills and processes that allow us to have a job - and then selling our time for money. Now part of the challenge in this stage is that the money was pretty good. It's easy to settle here and have a good life - but it didn't give me a great life. I was earning money, but it was at the expense of my freedom. I realized I could only get paid if I was seeing patients.

I started to see how I was tied to my profession. I was tied to being in the office all day, and it was emotionally draining as people came in day after day with their problems. It wasn't sustainable. I couldn't do it forever.

I didn't want a job - no matter how much it paid. I wanted freedom and autonomy. My dreams and the life that I had created weren't matching. The path I'd been encouraged to go down was well-trodden - but not a path that would lead me to freedom. So, I set the goal of finding a new path. I decided right then and there that I needed to figure out how to create my own financial freedom. I set the goal of becoming 'Financially Free at 33.'

Stage one is when we're earning an active income. We are essentially on a see-saw. We can reduce our hours to have more freedom - but our income will drop too. Or we lift our hours to earn more money - at the expense of our freedom. Active income isn't all bad - because the flip-side is that it provides an almost immediate and guaranteed income. If you work this week, you will get paid next week. That short-term reliability is what attracts so many people to active income opportunities. The long term of course - is that the second you stop doing the working tasks, so does your income.

I realized I needed to move into stage two and create leverage. I needed to get paid for other people's time too. I could only see twenty patients a day - so I figured the best way to improve my leverage was to go into small business ownership. I was able to bring in other employees who could see more patients and I was able to create some more flexibility in my life as well as generating extra income. But there was still a ceiling on my earnings. I was able to see more patients through our clinic thanks to having employees - but the expenses went right up too. I had to pay for employees, the building, and overheads. I had increased my income and had some extra flexibility, but it wasn't the freedom I was chasing.

So, I started to learn more about stocks, commodities, currencies, and property investment. With the extra income from my small business, I was able to buy a couple of investment properties, but the end game of freedom still seemed so far away. It takes time for investments to start making money. Their compounding effect is incredible, but it can take a little bit of time to get going. Based on my current situation, I would be fifty or sixty before I became financially free. I wanted to do everything I could to buy more investments to speed up the process, but there was a limit on what I could do.

I was frustrated and angry at this point. I was about to turn thirty, and I was doing everything people said you should do. I got a good degree, started a small business, and put money into investments. But it just felt like freedom was getting further away every week - not closer. And then came Network Marketing. The very last place I thought I would end up. But it showed up in my life, and everything I'd ever wanted suddenly seemed achievable. The missing link I was needing was here.

In network marketing, we love to talk about *residual income* and *financial freedom*; they are the exciting end games. But they're not immediate - they come further down the path. There's still a process to get there. Once we understand that and the opportunities and challenges of each stage - we can have a crystal clear road map to get to where we need to be.

Network marketing also has an active income - when we talk to people and bring them into our business. This is an active income because it's based on the work we do. Talk to lots of people - you'll be able to earn these bonuses. If you don't open your mouth - you don't get those much-awaited bonuses. And they are precisely that - a bonus. They're great, but we can't live a life of freedom off them. We have to remember they're just the first step. We can get caught up here thinking that once money starts coming in - it will keep coming in. But it's not residual yet. It's still stage one.

The next stage is being able to be paid on other people's time. Moving from an active income into leveraged income. This comes from duplication. Having systems and tools that allow the people we sponsor to also start creating their own active incomes. The deeper the systems duplicated - the more leverage we have and the faster we can accelerate our income. As much as we love to talk about residual income and freedom, this ability to create incredible leverage in a short space of time is what makes network marketing the best-kept secret in wealth creation.

In the real world, people regularly look to businesses to improve their leverage. Exactly the same thought process I had all those years ago. But there are huge costs associated with setting up a business. All the initial costs of finding a place, purchasing equipment, training staff etc. Then every week you need to pay rent products, marketing, wages, insurance etc. In Network Marketing we can avoid almost all of these costs. People can start their business for the cost of a starter pack. They can be earning active and leveraged income almost immediately without putting massive amounts of money into the business.

We also don't require people to have considerable knowledge of business to get started. People can come in without having to get a degree or expensive training. They can use scripts, and we plug them into templates and get started straight away. They are provided with strategies that anyone can use! As they follow the systems in place, they bring in customers and distributors themselves.

Being a small business owner, this was where I hit a brick wall. Significant leverage is almost impossible to create in a small business. There is only so much stuff you can fit under one roof. Only so many people will walk through the door each day. There would be huge financial implications with business expansion, and there was no guarantee it would even pay off.

This is where network marketing starts to surpass the standard business model by far. Network marketing offers us the fantastic gift of leverage through duplication. Think about tools like Zoom and Facebook. I can be on a Zoom call and talk to a thousand team members all at once worldwide. I can post on Facebook and get thousands of people to interact with a post and get excited to buy a product. I don't have to reach out to thousands of people individually and tell them about the next promotion. More people join the group - more people see the post. I don't have to reach out to them all individually. The best part is, I can get a percentage of the earnings when that product is bought!

I love leverage. But every strength can also be a potential weakness. And this is where I see so many people hitting a wall in their business. Because leverage can often masquerade as residual.

Tools and systems allow people to come in and, rapidly, follow a formula and start seeing results. This allows for a growing business and growing paychecks. BUT - at this point, the team is still made up of followers. They are dependent on you to provide the next tool. Dependent on you to run the Zoom call. Dependent on you to create the next promotion for the FB group. And when the team depends on your - there's no freedom. You can earn great amounts of money here, have huge momentum and change your income level fast. But running a team of dependent followers won't allow freedom. That only comes from creating independent leaders who can branch off and run their own teams.

We've all heard the saying - it's not what works; it's what duplicates. But duplication also requires people to follow a system. And we are then presented with this paradox - we want people to come in and follow the systems and tools, but we also want independent leaders who are creative and can think for themselves. Leaders, by definition, don't follow.

Leverage and residual can look similar. But they are not the same. Don't get them confused.

Duplication and leverage are fantastic, but to have true residual income (stage three), we need to identify the people who are built differently. Who are the square pegs in a round hole? The people who don't follow our systems - because they want to create their own. As much as they can be frustrating - they're also the exact people we need to take our business to the next level.

Now, let's be honest, most people are happy being led. They don't want to be independent, and they don't want to lead their own team. Most people want to be *part* of a team. They love the culture, and this will always be their side hustle - this is a little bit extra for them. They will follow the systems, be on team calls, and do the team challenges, which is exciting for them. And that's totally fine. We have systems, tools, groups, events, etc. for them. To take the next step we need to identify our potential leaders and put them in a separate room. They can't be systemized or duplicated. They're just not built that way. But that's also why they're so valuable.

> **Coach's Notes:**
>
> *Years ago, I hosted an event in Australia where my good buddy, Frazer Brookes, introduced me to Andrew Logan. We had known each other online and chatted a bit, but I didn't really know him. I was able to go to his amazing house, watch him train an audience of hundreds of network marketers from all different companies, and then have a private dinner with him and his wife, Angie. Here is what impressed me the most. Andrew gets leverage. He knows that leverage is necessary to build a big business, but he also knows leverage is critical to having a life. We all too often confuse being busy with being productive. Leverage helps us to focus truly, and Andrew is a master at teaching both money and mindset. He knows the key is massive leverage. Study the previous pages over and over again until you finally **get it** and live it.*

Creating leaders

Before we move into stage three and create leaders - a quick warning. People can often get themselves into big financial trouble at this point because they increase their lifestyle as rapidly as their income increases. They upgrade the car, the house, and start booking holidays. They think they have gotten to the residual stage, and they begin to live their lifestyle as such. They start taking more holidays, taking more time away from the business - and the money drops. They thought they had residual, but it was actually leverage - thanks to a dependent team.

The team was reliant on them to run the calls - so the calls stopped. The team was reliant on them to run the next blitz - so the blitzes stopped. And when the team stops working, the incomes start dropping - rapidly. This is where people can get really stuck. Their lifestyle has accelerated, and so have the expenses - but now their income is tumbling. And they're up the proverbial creek.

People can become 'leverage addicts' at this point. These people get caught up in one more blitz, one more push, one more promo. Searching for that next quick spike that can turn their business around. They're exhausting their team and their customers. Eventually, they're left with nothing. Don't become a "leverage addict."

I have had people come to me and say that they lost all of their money doing network marketing. And at first, I used to be so baffled. How? In most companies, you're starting your business for under $1,000. It isn't network marketing where they lost their money. It was the fact that they began to live a costlier lifestyle before they could sustain it. People start spending more and working less. They got caught up in potential and lost focus of the process. One day the checks dry up, or their team has moved on. Their safety net is gone. They blame network marketing, but really, it was their poor financial decisions that got them there.

As an industry, we can do so much better. So often people say that network marketing is a get rich quick scam - but also, sometimes we self-perpetuate that with how quickly we spend all of our money. How poorly we respect the process. We need to do better. If we helped more people understand this process, educate them on the different types of income and their strengths and weaknesses, and show them how to turn their money into wealth - then people will see our industry for the true diamond that it is.

Financial freedom is about taking care of your money. We are great at creating systems and showing people how to *make* money. But we need to get great at teaching people how to take *care* of money. If we want to provide a vehicle for financial freedom, we need to teach people financial skills.

Leverage is an incredible way to accelerate our income and earn more money. But we're not earning residual income until we have leaders who are branching off and running their own teams. So, it means that you need to step into the role of mentor instead of rock star.

Training and mentoring great people to become independent leaders takes time. It's not an overnight process. But that's also why it pays so well. The pay-off of long term residual income is incredible. That won't come without some work.

You have to show patience here. If you're searching for the quick spikes of the next blitz above - you're missing the long term value of mentorship. Part of the process here is actually getting out of your own way. Rather than focus on having one thousand people on your team call, focus on having ten people running their own one hundred people calls. Rather than ten thousand in your Facebook group, mentor five people to run their own 2 thousand person group. If you've done your job well, you should actually work yourself out of a job.

A person who has moved into the next phase focuses on the actual residual. They are mentors. They are focused on helping other people succeed and creating leaders on their team. What if we could develop leaders that are even better than we are? How amazing would that be? This is how residuals work. When we get out of our own way and start to create leaders, we are genuinely building success and freedom. If we genuinely want independence, we need to find the people that are hardwired differently. We have to find the people who want to eventually move away from being tied to us as the upline and sponsors.

I like to say it's a lot like raising children. We have two children that we absolutely love. They are the most important, beautiful, amazing people in the world to us. But we also want them to be able to live their own lives. We want them to be independent. We work hard every day to provide the best possible foundation for them. But if we never teach them how to take care of themselves and live their own lives, forging their own paths - then we have failed as parents.

It is the same with your team! We want our children to go out into the real world on their own, and the best way we can do that is by teaching them how to be independent. How to think for themselves, make their own decisions, stick with the consequences that come and learn from what happens.

Of all the systems in your business - the most important system is a way to identify those who want to follow, and those who want to lead. Who would like the templates to follow and who needs the space to grow? Who wants to be told what to do and who wants to do things first and learn after?

And it will be messy. They will absolutely make mistakes. However, it is all part of helping your leaders become independent and for you to truly move into residual income.

One of the most significant challenges of network marketing mentorship is finding leaders with the potential to grow. You need to give them a spot to get started, give them the systems and framework to launch, and then get out of the way and let them go and make their own systems and tools.

People love to talk about McDonalds as the gold standard for business systems. When people are buying a McDonald's, they aren't buying a franchise, they are buying their system (and the Real Estate). People are paying for a McDonald's franchise to learn how to put cheese, pickles, and onions on a sesame seed bun. Wherever you are in the world, every McDonald's uses the same system for putting together a hamburger. It's duplicated.

However, what's not as well known, is that the founder of McDonald's, Ray Kroc, had some franchise owners coming to him with their own ideas. They presented him with concepts like serving a breakfast menu and adding chicken burgers and nuggets to the beef range. Ray would listen and take on the most interesting ideas and develop them across the board for the entire business. Ray knew that he had intelligent people as franchise owners. So, he allowed these leaders to bring their ideas to him and then implemented them to make billions of dollars across the whole company.

With the McDonald's story, 96 percent of the franchise owners were happy to follow the systems, while the other 4 percent were drivers and dreamers. They were the ones coming to Ray with ideas, and you will see the same thing in your business. You will have 96 percent of people that will be doers. They will follow systems and be happy to have them. But when you find the 4 percent drivers, those are the leaders you will want to leverage. Your business needs this 4 percent. You will teach these people to think for themselves, and you will teach them *real* network marketing. Everyone else, you will teach systems.

Look for leadership character traits in people. Look for the people who are always coming up with ideas, always thinking of how things could be done differently. Look for the hustle and work ethic in people. The people who are always in action - without needing prompting or motivation. Identify these people and work with them 1:1. It's much easier to teach the skills of network marketing to drive people with great character traits, than trying to teach work ethic and innovation to someone who doesn't have any.

This may seem harsh, but to have true freedom, you need to identify these differences. Telling a doer to 'go out and just try things, make mistakes, fail lots of times - don't worry it's all part of learning' - that will scare them off. Telling a follower they could lead a team of thousands and how great that could be - will overwhelm them. They are struggling to lead in their own life, let alone a huge team of people. Conversely, telling a driver to just follow the systems and tools we have will frustrate and annoy them - and they'll quit.

There will be followers and people that will be dependent on us forever. We love them, and as I mentioned before, there is room for them in our business. But if you are focused on becoming free, there is no freedom in having everyone dependent on us. As long as we want freedom, we need to identify leaders and train them to run by themselves.

Coach's Notes:

*Are you a part of the 4 percent? Many say they want this business. Many say they need this business. Very few actually deserve the dream that they claim they want. Look, I believe you can deserve success. I believe we were all meant for more, but you have to go out and get it. You can't just think about it. As Andrew said, very few are **drivers**. Drivers don't make excuses. Drivers search for ways to win and do whatever it takes. Whatever your obstacles are, you can overcome them. As Andrew said, most won't be drivers. You are reading this book because you are or want to be a driver. Become the driver. Look for the drivers and create simple systems for 96 percent who are not drivers and are doers. Amateurs convince. Experts sift and sort.*

Bring on the passive income!

Finally, the last stage is passive income - putting a percentage of your money into investments. This is where we teach people about managing and multiplying their money. How to have their money out in the markets making more money. The most outstanding leaders teach us how to do life well. It's not just about helping them change their income - it's about helping people change their life.

The how-to of investing - well that's an impossible task to take on in one chapter. The important step is understanding the process and having a mindset of long term wealth from day one. As Rob says himself - *It's not a sprint or a marathon, it's both!*

There's nothing wrong with coming in with energy, action and urgency. Launching your business and helping people get started quickly. But don't lose sight of the long game as well. Don't forget that the sprints can help speed up the process, but they don't replace the process. If you try and sprint the whole way - you'll eventually collapse.

We want to build our business as quickly as possible - with skills and process as well as an excellent financial mindset and smart financial habits. Part of that is creating the habit of taking 5 to 10 percent of your income and putting it aside for investing. Doing this from day one. Create a habit today. Financial freedom isn't about having more money, it's about having better monetary skills. You don't magically learn about how to take care of your money just from earning more money.

Start creating long term financial habits today. If you want to speed up the process, and your income allows for it - put 20 to 50 percent of your money into this budget. The key here is to stay consistent. If you follow this system over three to five years, you will drastically change your family's future. How amazing is that! It's not just about the residual income. It's about becoming financially free.

That is how you become a great network marketer. An average leader leads followers. A good leader leads leaders. A great leader teaches people how to fully experience life.

My mantra is, "Teaching people to follow is duplication. Teaching people to think for themselves is reproduction. Reproduction creates a new generation". If you want generational wealth and freedom - work on creating a generation of leaders, who can create a generation of leaders.

We have the very best vehicle in creating financial freedom - as long as we show people the road map beside it. There's four stages to go through. Only four. Don't try to short-cut them. Every single person reading or listening to this book has the opportunity to be financially free. You just need to follow the map. Identify where you are, figure out the next step you need to take and get to work - and you can experience genuine financial freedom.

Coach's Notes:

Andrew is teaching you the next level of money mindset. Having your residual income make residual income from investments is the ultimate goal. Too many people lack this vision and discipline. They focus on the short-term lifestyle and sacrifice true long-term wealth. The goal isn't to look wealthy but to be wealthy. When wealth is done right, it represents all of your goals, dreams, and ambitions. When you can take care of your financial needs and put the proverbial oxygen mask on yourself first, then it is fantastic to help others. You can do it!

ANGIE GISCHEL

Achievements:

- Special needs momma and wife

- Joined Network Marketing at the age of forty-four in 2016

- Achieved Top Rank of the company in the first two months of business

- Built a team of over 10,000 members in eighteen months

- Personally recruited over 200 brand partners

- As an entrepreneur and social media marketer, her mission is to live a life of freedom, passion, and impact. In addition, to build generational wealth for her family and inspire others to do the same

"Start with your *why* and hold on with your Vision."

Building while working a full time corporate job

This is how you build your network marketing business while working a full-time corporate job.

October 23rd, 2014, I remember the exact moment that changed the course of my life and our family's future. What started as a routine pediatric wellness visit for our 16-month-old son turned into one of the most challenging days of our lives. To this day, I can still hear the exact words of our pediatrician as if I were sitting in the room. I still get choked up every time I remember. "I think your son may have Cerebral Palsy." I could not breathe. I could not talk. I could not even look at my husband, who was sitting in the room with us. I felt like I was in a bad dream.

We were given instructions on the steps to begin testing and walked out of that doctor's office feeling lost. It was the longest, quietest car drive home. We walked into our home, sat down, held our son and each other, and just cried. We did not know the outcome, but we knew we were in for a long journey. As a mom, I knew in my heart something was not exactly right. There were many delays in milestones, but I wasn't prepared to turn those thoughts into reality.

We spent the next few years going through testing and came up with zero answers. By July of 2016, I was feeling overwhelmed entirely. I worked a very demanding job in the pharmaceutical industry and felt guilty every time I needed to miss work for doctor's appointments. As much as I loved my career, I knew I needed something different. Something that would allow me the time I needed to be at all my son's appointments. I was also struggling with wanting to be home with him every day, not knowing the outcome of his diagnosis. I was desperate.

I knew there had to be a way, so I went to Big Brother Google and searched for work-at-home jobs. While I was combing through tons of opportunities and feeling lost, I noticed that a new friend on Facebook posted about her side gig. I reached out to her to see what she was doing and listened to a 20-minute recorded call. Immediately I caught the vision and signed up. I knew that if I stuck with it, I could work the business part-time and build it up to replace my full-time income so that I could be at home. My thought was, "If she can do it, I can do it, too."

Fast forward to November 2016, and we finally received a diagnosis for our son. Unfortunately, he has an exceedingly rare genetic disorder that may prevent him from ever being independent. As a result, my *why* became even more significant. With lots of hard work, struggles, and dedication, I more than replaced my pharmaceutical income and left the corporate world in April of 2020. I was now working my network marketing business full-time. My ultimate goal shifted from replacing my corporate income to creating generational wealth so that my son will always have the best care for the rest of his life.

I know people struggle to understand and even believe how leaving a corporate job is possible. We get stuck feeling like it is the only way to make money, but the lifestyle doesn't match what we ultimately want. As much as I loved my corporate job, it wasn't helping me best support our family the way we all needed to be supported. I was making money but where I needed to be was with my son. Network marketing changed all of that for me.

I will share some key components that I believe are necessary for you to build your network marketing business while working a full-time corporate job. Whether you want to create a supplemental income or go full-time in network marketing, these key components will help you along your journey.

Coach's Notes:

"Does your why make you cry" is a common cliché in the network marketing space. Angie sure does. Let me rephrase. Is your why stronger than your objections? Is your why stronger than your mood swings? We all go through trials in our lives and our businesses. At the beginning of one's network marketing journey, one's why typically isn't big yet. They typically just want to make their money back and then their why expands and grows. Eventually, you must create a reason big enough to push you through those days, weeks, months, quarters, and years when you just don't feel like it. Angie had such a desire to make something work that she sought it out and made it work!

Decide now!

You need to *decide.*

Your why is one of the first things that you need to figure out, and it needs to be so solid that no matter what obstacles come at you, you stay on course to reach your goals. Now, you may feel like you do not have "a why that makes you cry" like mine, but I promise that you have something that will pull you through the ups and downs of building a business. Write down why you decided to start a network marketing business and why it is important to you. Keep it somewhere you can see it at all times. You must determine what your why is and be reminded of it constantly.

After five years of being in the industry and trying a few different companies, it was not until 2020 that I was able to earn a six-figure income and leave the corporate world. So many people have come to me and asked me what I did to achieve that goal. I had to sit down and have a heart-to-heart with myself. I had to figure out what I did differently this time that I had not done in other companies. What brought me the success I had been looking for?

I decided.

Although I had told myself that I was doing everything I could to build my business, I realized that even though I had achieved some success, I was always moving two steps forward and one step back. As you build your network marketing business, you will come across people who laugh at your goals, make negative comments about your business, try to distract you from your dreams, tell you what you are doing does not work, and you will face rejections, etc. I know this from experience as I ran into these obstacles myself. As soon as I started gaining momentum in my business, an obstacle would get in my way, and I would second guess what I was doing. Therefore, you must put blinders on and keep pushing forward.

In January 2020, I decided that nothing and no one would stop me from reaching my goals - I had a mindset shift. As much as you tell yourself that you are 100 percent dedicated to your goals, you still have one foot out the door until you have that shift. And if you have one foot out the door, it may as well be closed. When you are an independent entrepreneur, you must believe in what you are doing relentlessly to succeed. So, make the decision. Fight for your goals. Fight for your family. Embrace the challenges and learn from the lessons.

Coach's Notes:

*Angie just simplified the success formula in one word: **decide**. When you decide on success, everything else falls into place. When you decide, the **how** will eventually show itself. Think of the word decide. The second part of that word is "cide." That word is often associated with "kill." Think of Suicide, Homicide, Pesticide, and even Decide. To decide is to kill the option. It is to make that commitment truly. In large part, your level of commitment will determine your level of success.*

Set your goals

You must set goals and take consistent daily action to achieve them. You cannot build a business on hope.

I hope I get a new customer today.

I hope I get a new business partner today.

I hope I hit that rank I want this month.

When you are building your business part-time, you must be diligent with your goals and how you will achieve them. Setting goals is one of the most important keys to being successful when you work for yourself. Setting goals keeps you focused and moving toward achieving what you want out of your business.

First, set yourself long-term goals. Where do you want to be in your business in one year, five years, or ten years? What rank do you want to achieve? How much income do you want to earn? Set these goals to be big enough to be a little scary and give you the drive to take action every day. If you make these goals too small, they will not inspire you or motivate you.

For instance, my big long-term goal was to leave my 9 to 5 job and develop a full-time network marketing business while replacing my income. While this was exciting for me, it was also scary. I have known nothing except to work, punch a time clock, and depend on someone else to pay for my efforts. I did not realize before network marketing that if I put the same effort and determination into a business, I could determine my worth. So do not be afraid to make those big audacious goals. Write them down somewhere where you can see them every single day.

Next on the list is to set short-term goals. For example, when you are thinking about how much money you want to earn in a year or what rank you want to be, you want to write down what that will take and break that down into smaller goals. For example, if you're going to make $50,000 a year in your network marketing business, how much would you need to make monthly, weekly, daily to achieve that goal. This will help you see what it will take to hit the bigger goal for the year. You then can look at your compensation plan and figure out exactly how many sales you need to make or how much volume your team needs to generate for you to hit those daily, weekly, and monthly goals, and then your yearly goal will follow. This is called reverse engineering your goals and will become valuable to you part-time as you work this business.

Manage your time

Now that you have your goals set, it is time to get to work! I figured out that I did not need more time to build the successful business of my dreams. What I needed was to be more efficient and productive with the time that I had. You need to learn how to build your business part-time to show others how to do it. If you will teach someone how to do something and have never done it yourself, why would they listen to you?

Teaching someone something you have done before makes you relatable. It also shows them that it's an achievable goal. Preparation is key. Before I fired my boss and went full-time into network marketing, if I did not plan my week out, I would be exhausted when I got home from work and would not get as much done as I wanted to. So being strategic in planning your week is essential. So, pick a day to do that. If you work Monday through Friday, take Sunday to prepare for your week.

Plan your content for the entire week. How many posts will you make, and what topics will you cover? On what days will you be posting? Have this all pre-planned.

Plan your reach-outs for the week. If your goal is to reach out to five people a day, then write down on your list the 35 people you are going to reach out to during the week. Having your plan for the week will keep you from burnout. Can you get more production out of the limited time you have? You probably can with a bit of planning.

Here is what a typical day for me looked like. When I was working full time, I was commuting two to three hours a day, working 8 to 10 hours a day, and still needed time with my family. So, I needed to become very efficient with the time I had available. So, my car became a mobile office. I spent my commute talking to my team, talking to new prospects, and following up with potential customers and brand partners.

I would also use my commute time to self-develop. Leaders are readers, or in my case, leaders are listeners. I self-developed every day for 15 to 30 minutes a day without fail. Amazon audio books became my best friend. And if I did not have a book that I wanted to listen to, I would head to YouTube. I would notate the book or video if I heard a tip or strategy I wanted to utilize in my business. Then, when I had time in the evening or on the weekend, I would go back to that book, write down the tip or strategy, and implement it into my business. Reading and learning are great, but you are wasting your time if you are not executing what you are learning.

Once I arrived at work, I had very little time to work on my network marketing business, so I had to get creative. Thanks to Fraser Brooks, I took his *building from the bathroom* tip and ran with it! I would take my phone to the bathroom with me and utilize that time to answer messages from my team, answer questions from prospects, and send tools to prospects. Whatever it may have been that I could do in a text message, it would get done in the bathroom. So, if anyone from my team is reading this, chances are you have talked to me from the loo.

I also utilized my breaks and lunches to work my business. Now would I rather have sat around the table with my friends and gossiped about work and coworkers and what the company could do and not do to make things better for the employees? Would I rather listen to them talk about how much fun they had over the weekend and their plans for the weekend coming up? Of course! And there were lots of times when my friends would laugh at me because they would say something that caught my attention just to catch my attention and then laugh at me about being on my phone and not knowing what they were talking about.

But when you have goals and dreams that will require your time, there are some sacrifices that you have to make. As much as I love my friends, my why was the most important thing to me, and it was what drove me every day to make sacrifices to achieve my goal.

Prospecting and marketing

Since I joined the industry in 2016, the concept of attraction marketing has grown astronomically. It's grown to the point that some are teaching this as the only way to build your business. If you are teaching your team to only attract people to them and to not prospect (reach out to) potential business partners and customers, you are doing them a disservice, in my opinion. Using the *post and pray strategy* may take you an exceptionally long time to build your business to the level you desire.

Don't get me wrong; I think attraction marketing is excellent. Who does not want people reaching out to them every day asking them about their product or service? Building your business using this strategy is possible, but it is a much slower build unless you have high influence. I believe you should be prospecting alongside marketing if you want to utilize the part-time hours you have to build your business most productively. Your time is already limited, so why wouldn't you use every tool in your toolbox?

If you have a limited amount of time to complete an income-producing activity, that activity should be prospecting. For example, if you have 10 minutes available, you should be prospecting for eight of those 10 minutes. If you have 30 minutes available, you should be prospecting a minimum of 20 minutes. You need to be very strategic and do the activities that bring the most value to your business.

Marketing is a very crucial component to building your business; hence, network **marketing**. Combining marketing with prospecting is the fastest way to get more eyes on you and what you have to offer to your network. If you are properly marketing on your social media and have conversations with people daily, it will encourage them to ask what you are doing. Now I am not referring to spamming people, sending people your links without their approval, or cold messaging. I am talking about conversations.

One of the statements that I have heard in our industry repeatedly is you must become a professional conversation starter. I cannot tell you how often I have reached out to someone in messenger to say hello or give a genuine comment about a post that they made that led to them ask me about something they saw in one of my posts. Sometimes people are too busy when they see your post to ask you, or sometimes, they are afraid to message you. But, when you genuinely converse with people, it opens the door.

Find a mentor.

I will never tell anyone that this is an easy business or that it was easy for me to build a business to the level I needed to quit my 9 to 5 corporate job. It is not easy, but it is simple. However, you will have challenges with your belief in yourself, the industry, products or services, the company, etc. You will have obstacles along your journey, and so it is vital to have a mentor. Find someone who inspires you when you are feeling low - someone experienced in the industry and someone who shares valuable tips and strategies on building your business. You need someone who provides positive energy and helps you stay when times are challenging. Having the right mentor or mentors will play a big part in your success.

Rob Sperry did not know who I was for years, but I knew who he was. Rob was my mentor long before he invited me to take part in this book. I found Rob through another network marketing coach and loved his style. He coaches with real strategy but can also be funny and inspiring at the same time. In addition, he does a phenomenal job sharing what our incredible industry can provide regarding time freedom and having the quality time and adventures with the family that I strongly desired. So, I am completely honored that Rob invited me to be part of his book. And I hope that I have inspired you or shared some strategy that helps you attain your dreams and goals in your network marketing business.

You really can replace and exceed what you are making in the corporate world. You can have the lifestyle and the money that you have always wanted. If you can remember these tips and implement them fast, you will see your results start to exceed what you thought was even possible.

Coach's Notes:

Again, Angie gave you the simplified success formula as well as a more advanced one. Well done! Now go back and challenge yourself. Ask yourself this: on a scale of 1 to 10, how well am I doing on:

- Deciding (sticking to a commitment)
- Setting goals
- Managing your time
- Prospecting and marketing
- Finding a mentor

*As you assess these, start with at least one of them and **decide** to become better at it!*

ARIELLA HENDERSHAW

Achievements:

- Team of over 5,000 stylists
- Reached $30million in team volume in three years
- Top Recruiter in 2019
- Currently studying Leadership at Cornell University

Quote:

"They whispered to her, 'You cannot withstand the storm.'"

"She whispered back, "I am the storm."

How to SMASH those objections

I was at a point in my life where I had no idea what to do career-wise. I was a young entrepreneur, and I had just sold my Performing Arts Studio, which was open for eight years. I was ready for something new.

Enter Recruiting. I loved talking with people and building relationships, and when a recruiting position at a very well-known insurance company opened up, I applied. I was hired and started immediately. I had no idea what recruiting entailed, but I knew I would be good at it because I was hungry! I was hungry for success. So, there I was, cold calling at least one hundred people per day and finding resumes on whatever online resume tool I could find! You see, I accepted a low salary with the hopes of earning a bonus for each agent that I hired. But the more I did it, the more I realized that this was *hard*!

As I was making all these calls, I noticed something interesting. Many people were willing to chat with me. I would introduce myself, ask them a bit about themselves and tell them why I was calling. I would explain the job, and then it would happen. They would ask the most feared question. They would ask what the starting salary was.

Silence.

Why was there silence? This position that I was hiring for did not come with a salary, or benefits, or anything. It was commission only. And once they heard those two words (commission only), they hung up—one by one. And after being hung up on 100 times per day, five days a week, I felt defeated. What was I doing wrong?

I must've not been the only one struggling because a couple of months later, the company started training their recruiters on one subject: Objections.

We were to report to the conference room every day for two weeks. And what was the focus of those meetings? Roleplaying objections. Brilliant! So, what did I learn by roleplaying objections with my co-workers for *hours* on end? Objections aren't as scary as they seem! There is no reason to back down and fear an objection because once you practice them and start having the same ones said to you repeatedly, you stop making it about yourself and start seeing it as other people requesting more information! The "no" isn't personal anymore. Don't fear the objections. Enjoy the initial conversation because, within that, you can gather so much information about that person to help you *smash* those objections!

Coach's Notes:

One of my favorite parts about these kinds of books is getting a more in-depth perspective from different top leaders. Ariella went through what most of us would perceive as a painful type of job. Cold calls! 100 people a day. That would have been my nightmare, but she used this experience to **learn** *and* **grow***. She used it to combat her fears. She realized that objections don't have to be scary. In fact, objections can be a great thing. It means they are interested and give you all the information they require to get a yes.*

Is it really a no?

A "no" isn't always a "no." Sometimes it's just a question of "Tell me more. Give me more information. I want to hear more." What makes a "no" so hard to hear is that we think it is an absolute. We believe that when someone says "no" to us, they are *rejecting* us. We understand "no" to mean that we can never speak to this person again or that they will never change their mind.

One way to *smash* the objection is to get curious about the "no." When you hear the objection, ask yourself if there is anything else that the person in front of you needs to know. See if they need more education, or more time, or more questions answered. Remember that the "no" can also mean "not right now." I can't tell you how many times I have heard a "no," but when I circle back around, they have changed their mind, and that person has joined the business. So, stop thinking about "no" as an absolute.

Coach's Notes:

No, sometimes means, "I don't know enough." Ariella has had many successes, from a "no" turning into a "yes." The one person that helped my personal business more than anyone else said "no" to me the first time I approached him. Don't give up on people. Don't misinterpret what Ariella or I am saying. That doesn't mean you pester someone who isn't interested. Instead, follow what Ariella is about to teach you.

100 people

Imagine that you have a room full of one hundred people. You hold up your insurance card and ask, "Who wants a job selling insurance?" You may have two to three people who are all in to start working with you right away. Are you going to be offended that the other ninety-seven people didn't raise their hands? No! You don't know why they didn't raise their hands. You need to ask more questions and see what is holding them back from being all in and saying "yes." People usually say "no" because they don't have enough information. Objections are *your opportunity* to get them more information.

This opportunity may not be for everyone. Once again, that has nothing to do with you. Once I have given them all the information about working in the insurance industry, there may be people there that say, "I already have a job." or "Insurance is a scam." It's okay for them to have their opinion and say "no." However, I never know when this person may *not* have a job. If I make sure that I give them the information, they may be back in that room next week asking to work with me. Remember, people's situations can change. Part of smashing objections is learning what information to present and when to deliver it. Just like the insurance analogy, network marketing isn't for everyone. Yes, everyone *can* do it, but not everyone wants to do it. *And that's okay!*

Overcoming objections method

I have learned one of the best methods to overcome objections with any sales business. Once I realized this, I felt like it didn't matter what objection someone had; I would have the answer. It is called the "feel, felt, found" method. This method is brilliant in overcoming objections, so let's get right into it. As people bring up objections, you will use emotion and your own experience to validate what they are saying, acknowledge it, and give them a solution.

Here is the framework. Let's say you just got an objection from someone. You are going to say I hear that you are *feeling* this way. I have *felt* that way too. What I have *found* is this_____. The best part is that you are not making their objection a big deal. You aren't taking it on to be personal. You allow the person to have their objection and give them a solution for getting out of it.

Let me use an example that happened on my team. There is a woman on my team named Patricia. She was currently hosting a party for me but hadn't yet signed up to start her own business. I met with her and mentioned that her sales at the party were through-the-roof amazing. She was earning hostess rewards but not getting a paycheck because she wasn't yet part of the business. I asked her if she had ever considered joining the company. She said, "Yes, I have. I love the product, and my friends do, too. I love getting together with people, and it seems like such a fun thing. The only problem is that I don't have time."

Are you guys ready to *smash* that objection with me? Here was my response. Pay attention! All I did was use the *feel, felt, found* method.

"Thanks for sharing that with me." (Validate her feelings)

"I know how it can *feel* loving something and seeing the potential, but not *feeling* like you have any time to pursue it. I *felt* that way, too, when

49

I first started with network marketing. I *felt* like I would never have enough time to build the business and make money because I was a new mom, and my husband worked full time. But what I *found* was that I could run this business whenever I wanted to! My son took naps throughout the day, so I spent 10 minutes each day connecting with customers. So, it really only took me a couple of hours on the weekend or nights to make some great income."

I then gave her some more information about what that would look like for her life.

Patricia joined the business that night and has been doing fantastic with the company ever since. Now, think about this. What would have happened if I would have let the objection stop the conversation? Where would my business be if every time someone had an objection, I gave up? I definitely wouldn't be at the top of my company, and I definitely would not make anywhere near the paycheck I am making right now. You have got to stop taking objections so personally.

When you believe the objection

One major setback with objections is when my team believes the objection themselves. For example, let's say someone comes and says, "My husband will get mad at me." If the person making the offer also has a husband who may get mad, she suddenly agrees and gives up the sale. You have to remember that your collective experience with the person in front of you is no reason *not* to overcome their objections.

I can't imagine what my life would be like if my sponsor (hey girl!) had given me a pass because of our shared story. I was definitely the woman that had all the objections in the world. But that didn't stop her from inviting me to join her and overcoming all of my objections. I am so glad she did, too, because I wouldn't be here today without her doing the work.

Because of that, I have told myself that no one's objections are worth sacrificing their potential. I had a mom I was talking to, and she mentioned that she couldn't do this because she just had a baby and felt like it was too hard. Once again, I used my story because I had been there.

When I started this business, I had just had a new baby that was four months old. I was going through postpartum depression, and I felt like I couldn't handle everything going on. I was overwhelmed. As this woman told me her objections, I knew I wanted to give her every opportunity to smash through her own objections and show up for herself. I did the *feel, felt, found method*, and it worked.

We had a fantastic conversation about what it's like to be a struggling newborn mom and work through depression. We talked about starting a business and the confidence it helped me build. We talked about the community she would be joining. We talked about what was possible for her life. This all happened because I used the *feel, felt, found* method with her objection.

The fantastic thing about network marketing is that you can build your business and build your empire, one objection at a time. You can listen to anything someone uses as an objection and know that you have an answer to smash through it. You know that nothing anyone says can stop you. One question I get is, "What do I say if I have never experienced something like the objection that someone gives me? What if I can't relate?"

Great question! Start using other people. Use your team, use your sponsor, use someone else's story that you heard in the company. It doesn't always have to be your "found story." You will do it precisely the same way. "I can see how you *feel* that way. My sponsor *felt* that way too. This is what my sponsor *found* ____."

Another thing I hear my team say is, "Is smashing through objections forcing someone to join the business?" No, absolutely not. When we smash through objections, what we are doing is giving people an opportunity to say "yes" confidently. We are letting them know that it doesn't have to be a "no." They can overcome the objection and say yes. Again, going back to the insurance example, we know that some people will still say "no" regardless of how well we smash their objections. That's okay. The *feel, felt, found* method is all about letting the person in front of you know that it can be a "yes" if they want it to be.

Some tips to become a pro at smashing through objections: First, practice makes perfect. Start practicing with your team and look for opportunities to use this method. Practice *a lot*! Second, don't make them personal. Third, never get defensive, condescending, or forceful during the objection. And finally, collect stories. Use your own stories, use your team's stories, and use your sponsor's stories.

I know where you are at right now with your business. I have been there. I remember feeling like I wanted this business to work, but I questioned if I was the type of person that could be successful. It felt scary and exciting to believe what my sponsor said and go all-in on myself and my business. I found that when I dropped the fear of what other people would think and the story that I didn't know enough, I became motivated and driven to make this happen. The more I focused on my growth and my team's growth, the more successful I became. I know that you can do it too! Just the fact that you are reading this book means that you can do this. So go out and make it happen for yourself, and don't let any objection stand in your way!

P.S. Did you see what I did there?! I told you it works!

Coach's Notes:

Handling objections takes time. Instead of getting frustrated, take what Ariella has laid out for you as your objection guide. No matter how good your training is, you can't learn it unless you implement it. You can't become a professional pianist from watching YouTube videos and not actually playing the piano - you have to **implement!** *Go, take action, and chase those dreams.*

ASHLEY STANLEY

Achievements

- Network Marketing Multi-Millionaire
- 10 Year Industry Expert, Trainer, and Entrepreneur Advocate
- Leader of 6,000+ Distributors
- 140,000 Customers
- Dominator of Brand Clarity and Business Building
- Former Exercise Physiologist/Personal Trainer earning two and a half times her corporate salary
- Creator of the LUXE Collection, featuring female empowerment apparel and products

Quote:

"Who loses if you don't win?"

- Danelle Delgado

Let's Get Visible... Using Video to Increase Sales and Sponsoring

Hey y'all! I'm Ashley…Mom, Wife, lover of Alien Shows, Fast Cars, and Residual Income. My goal for this chapter is not to teach how to be the best and most perfect person on video…my goal is to empower you to start learning to use video in all your imperfect glory! So, let's get this party started.

Why is using video in your business so important? Well, as cliché as it sounds, video can change people's lives. I know that because about four years ago, it changed mine. I was in the middle of transitioning network marketing companies, and I kept seeing this guy's videos pop up. For one, I was wondering why the heck no one had taught me these valuable strategies for my business and secondly, my fascination grew because I knew he was involved in a business but the way he presented the information didn't raise my resistance at all to what he was doing. The videos weren't "spammy" and they provided a ton of value to me. Ultimately those videos helped me find my new company. I started to learn how to do videos myself, and I inevitably began to recruit more business partners and sell more products. However, the process was so far out of my comfort zone that there were many times that I wanted to hide under a rock. Can you relate?

If I could pick a theme song for this chapter, it would be Drake - Started From The Bottom.

Before we really dive into this chapter, let's break the ice a little and debunk the myth that the people you see crushing it in any area of their life, on social media, or in their videos, magically started out as the version of them that you see today.

Being a beginner at something is super uncomfortable but, being completely unprepared can feel scary, embarrassing, and awkward AF. Kind of like that time I tried out for College Cheerleader, except for the fact that I had never been a cheerleader before. I'll save you the gory details but, I'm pretty sure my sub-par "performance" at tryouts left a gym full of Cheer Moms scarred for life after they determined that no one was going to jump out and announce that they were on some kind of practical joke

show. It was pretty bad to put it mildly. Did I make the squad? Ummmm…
No. Did I throw in the towel and give up? Also No…I kept going,
learned from my mistakes, and the sting of embarrassment and what I
was positive was social suicide faded into just a memory on what became
an exciting journey that led to 2 Collegiate National Championships
and valuable lessons that have served me well in life and business.
The Moral of that story is this…wherever you are on your journey
to building a six-figure business, there will be times when you might
embarrass yourself or even question if this is actually for you. IT IS!
Keep going, because the struggle makes success that much sweeter.

Ashley's Story

Before I got started in network marketing, I was well on my way to success
and living happily ever after…according to society…insert eye roll here.
I graduated College, got married, landed a great job, and had two kids.
I was living the dream, except I wasn't. I was miserable. Although my
husband had a great job in the Oil and Gas Industry, and financial stress
was not something that we experienced very often, our life was not what
we had envisioned for our kids or ourselves. I would often go weeks at
a time without seeing my husband and the kids without seeing their
dad. At the same time, Carter watched our children grow up through
pictures on his phone while he was on a drilling location. It was hard for
him to miss out on holidays, birthdays, anniversaries, and most of the
kids' first words, steps, and anything else you can imagine. I remember
sitting there with two small kids, thinking "This can't be what the rest
of our life is going to be like." I knew I had to do something. I didn't
know how I would do it or what it would look like, but I knew that I
could make it happen. And in that moment my mind became open to
possibilities I had never considered before.

At the time, I was working full time as an Exercise Physiologist and Personal Trainer. I knew that if I wanted to change the trajectory of our lives, I would have to make a substantial amount of income. Even with a College Degree and one of the best paying jobs in my area, I needed more. Around that time, I got invited to a home party for "one of those pyramid things." I went from skeptical to ALL IN in that one meeting. I was instantly attracted to the opportunity, the lifestyle, and the income potential. I had no idea what it meant to be in network marketing, but it was like someone had opened the door to the rest of my life. And just like that I was on my way. I joined the business, and the rest is all Lambos and beach vacays, right? Almost…but not quite.

When I joined Network Marketing, we had a six-year-old and a brand new baby. Getting in front of a room full of people was not my idea of a good time, but it was way less painful than the life we were living. I knew I could get through anything and make it work if it meant that Carter would be able to spend more time at home and less time on a drilling rig.

Here is what I want to share with you. This business is uncomfortable, especially at first. You are going to have to learn new skills and do things you have never done before. But, it is a small price to pay to live the kind of lifestyle that you are dreaming of. And I know you have BIG dreams. If you didn't, you wouldn't be reading this book right now. So, before we go any further, ask yourself…Am I willing to make that tradeoff? To learn new things? To live in discomfort? Because that my friend is where the real growth happens.

Like I mentioned before, when I started network marketing, home parties were all the rage. But as we have built our business, the business landscape has changed from in-person to online. And with that came the importance of using video. When I talk about the importance of video, I am specifically talking about utilizing the different types of videos available on various social media platforms.

It doesn't matter whether it's Facebook, Instagram, TikTok, or YouTube. Almost every platform has several options for sharing videos. You can share something Live, record short video clips in your stories, or you can pre-record and upload it to the site. You can even drop it like it's hot to your favorite song while still providing massive value to your audience. Go wild! After all, most platforms are entirely free for you to use. You can literally start marketing your business, right now, without spending a dime!

So how exactly does video help with your business? I'm so glad you asked. Video helps create a human connection that doesn't always exist in a digital world. Video has been crucial in the last two years as people worldwide seek new ways to expand and stay connected. We are no longer limited to our hometown or a local audience. We don't need to know people personally to connect with them. Social Media allows us to reach people all over the world, and video gives us a sense of who someone is even if we aren't talking to them face to face.

Coach's Notes:

Video is by far the most uncomfortable way to build a business and yet by far the most lucrative. Ashley is a total superstar, and by watching her videos now, you would never guess that she dreaded doing them. The difference between her and the non-successful is that she was willing to do whatever it took, including videos. Stop making excuses about why you can't do videos and just start. You will be bad at first, but that will create an even more powerful story later.

Everyone a convert

I have yet to find a faster, more effective way to convert followers into customers or business partners than by using video. Video helps create relatability and develops the Know, Like, and Trust factor like no other.

And the more someone relates to you, knows you, likes you, and trusts you, the more likely they are to buy into you, your offer, your products, your business, or your brand.

And before you go getting all hard on yourself because maybe you aren't great at videos yet, think about this… What was the last video that you really connected with on social media? Was it a pre-scripted video with a perfectly polished script? Probably not. In my opinion, the most impactful videos are the ones where one person shows up in all of their imperfectness, in hopes of impacting another.

And while we are on the topic of scripted videos, you may be wondering how the heck are you supposed to memorize content for an entire video. You're not. Well, I don't at least. When I do videos, I almost always have notes that I use as prompts. That's just who I am. I do better when I have a piece of paper in front of me with important points that I don't want to leave out. Many times, you will see me look at my notes during a video and I often announce that I am, in fact, looking at my notes. Who cares? Not my followers. They know that about me!

Coach's Notes:

*I wish I had known this earlier. I wish I could have read this part of the book ten years ago. I was so stuck on what to say on social media that I pretty much didn't do one video during my first five years in network marketing. I was overthinking it instead of just showing up and failing forward. When you are nervous, then spin that to a positive. People will relate to it because it is real. When your video is awful, use it as part of your learning experience and story. The point is to get started and just be **you**. You will learn as you go, and you will eventually become great. Don't allow your excuses of not starting well to prevent you from going after your dreams. You won't be good at first. Almost no one is, and that's okay! I permit you to **fail forward**.*

You Can BE YOU

I would like to preface this next part with the following statement… the best and most authentic version of yourself is always good enough. There is no need to be anyone other than YOU. If or when you meet someone in person, you want your offline self to match your online self. My worst nightmare would be to meet one of my business partners in person for the first time and have them be disappointed that they didn't get the online version of me. I don't want to burst their video bubble! I want them to feel like they already know me through my videos. That is one of the most crucial reasons to show up on video as your truly authentic self.

Like we talked about at the beginning of this chapter, being a beginner can be uncomfortable. Everyone starts with varying degrees of experience with video and social media platforms. I see it every time I bring a new person onto the team. Where most video beginners get stuck is in their perception of what is valuable to other people. We all get in our heads about not knowing what to share or thinking that we don't know enough or aren't "qualified" to be providing value to other people.

By now, you're probably thinking "what the heck am I even supposed to be talking about in these videos?" This can be a paralyzing thought for video newbies, so let me help put your mind at ease. Contrary to what you may have seen on Social Media, not everything has to be about your product or business. In fact, some of the most viral videos are things like a genius hack for cutting up a pineapple. Was the video complicated, fancy, or perfectly scripted? Nope! They weren't doing anything crazy. It was just a simple hack to cut a pineapple. Never underestimate the value of helping people save time and make complicated tasks less complicated. Don't overthink your videos, just press play and learn as you go.

I want to offer you a shift in perspective just in case you are still feeling under qualified in the area of teaching your way to those six figures that are so very possible for you.

So many people want to be the most knowledgeable trainer or the next big network marketing Guru. However, only about 5% of people in network marketing will create a massive income from becoming gurus and social influencers. That means there are 95% of people that need real, authentic videos about growing a business. They need the basic tips and real life. They need people who can serve as authentic teachers sharing tools that are actually helpful. Many times, things that you think everyone already knows or that may seem like common knowledge to you are the very things that can put someone on the path to a six figure business.

Tip of the CENTURY…write this one down, circle it, read it 10 times… Don't oversaturate your posting with selling. Think of it this way; when you're using video, you're providing value. People find it valuable whether you are teaching them about a product, sharing tips to grow their business, what it's like working from home, providing advice on living a healthier lifestyle, or my personal favorite…making them laugh. You can share general education, lessons you have learned, or something about your day-to-day life. Variety is the spice of life…and in this case, videos. Use variety to keep your audience's attention and interest high. My philosophy is this…the more value you provide, the more valuable people will find you.

If you ever want a good laugh or a confidence boost just head on over to my Facebook page and scroll back to my very first video. Lighting… Terrible. Content…Not amazing. Vibe…Awkward AF. When I first started doing videos, I was terrified to even push the button to go LIVE. When I did work up the courage to go LIVE, sometimes I would get so off track, that before I knew it, my train of thought had derailed past the point of no return. And as crazy as it sounds, sometimes I would even "lose my Wi-Fi signal" and my Live Video would "mysteriously" end right in the middle of me talking…so weird! When in reality, I got so flustered I would just end the video, delete it, and try again later. It's fine, I'm fine, everything is fine! It didn't have any sort of long term, negative impact on the effectiveness of my videos. I wanted to share this to let you know that it's okay to mess up. It's okay to completely bomb your video. You should be proud because you showed up and did it anyway!

Speaking of bombing, I was once doing a video, and my dog unexpectedly came stampeding into the room, making his Social Media Video Debut. He Form Tackled my ring light, sending my phone flying one way and my tripod the other. From my audience's point of view, I could only imagine that what they were seeing on screen looked more like the Blair Witch Project than the Live Video they thought they tuned into. It was far from perfect. In fact, I almost deleted it, but they loved it! I got so many messages that allowed me to start new conversations. Why? Because it was real! And that's what people relate with.

Okay, enough story time…

One of the hardest things for people to do besides pressing the record button, is learning to use their Social Media for Income and not Entertainment. This learning curve can be a difficult one and I would love to help you shorten it so that your videos can begin to help you increase your sales and even to sponsor more people.

Here are a few things that you can expect to happen when you start using videos for business. And since I'm not in the business of telling people what they WANT to hear, I'm going to shoot you straight…

1. The only truly bad video is the one that you don't do. There could be many exceptions to this tip but, for the sake of the word count in this chapter, we won't go there.

2. You will most likely not be amazing right away. If you are, congratulations, you should have been sharing your greatness with the world far before now.

3. Your regular audience may not resonate with the new way that you are using your Social Media Platform (i.e. – for income and not entertainment). They can have an opinion about what you do when they are the ones paying your bills.

4. You may lose followers…it's okay, those aren't your people! Your people are coming…trust me!

5. You may get mocked…but you aren't going to give up because in 10 years when you have time freedom and are free of financial stress, that won't even matter.

6. You are going to face judgments. There will be trolls and downright unhappy people that will make unflattering and embarrassing comments. It's not your job to argue, explain, or justify what you are doing…you are not the Jackass Whisperer! Delete, Block, Release, and keep going!

When you know what's coming, it's so much easier to take it for what it is and move on.

Let's talk about Likes, Comments, Views, etc…you know…the Vanity Metrics! Here is my strategy for Vanity Metrics…crumble them up into a little ball and throw them right out the window. No really! Focus on being a person of value to your audience and the "likes" and "comments" will come. Don't give up because you assume that people don't like what you're saying because you aren't getting the kind of engagement that you want. Stay consistent and it will come!

This next part because it left such an impression on me, and I wish I could remember where I read it so I could say thank you. But, since I can't, the next best thing I can do is share it with you in hopes that it might help you as much as it did me.

If you have twenty views, you fill up a classroom of people.

If you have one hundred to three hundred views, you fill up a movie theater.

If you have five hundred views or more, you fill up an auditorium.

And while those numbers may seem minimal in a digital world, if you were standing in front of three hundred people, you would see how many people you are actually impacting.

One view turns into ten, that turns into hundreds, that turns into thousands, millions, and beyond...but only if you keep going! You never know what you might say that could have the most profound and lasting effect on people's lives and businesses

Before we wrap this party up, I want to share with you what I say out loud before each video, teaching, or training that I do... "I don't have to be perfect; I just have to be me." It allows me to reassure myself that the right people will like what I'm saying, they will find value in what I'm putting out there, and that even if I only Impact one person, it's totally worth feeling uncomfortable for just a few minutes. Give it a shot next time you record something and let me know how it goes.

In closing, don't worry about the views, your voice, your hair, or anything that might stop you from pressing that play button. You never know who needs to hear what you have to say, it may even change their life, even if they don't realize it yet.

Perfection is the thief of confidence and progress so move forward imperfectly in everything that you do!

Coach's Notes:

One part that really hit home for me from these last few paragraphs was the following. "When people start posting videos, they get very involved with the likes and comments on the video. Stop it. Really. It's not about how many you get. It's about staying consistent and building an audience. The likes and comments will come."

*Don't do the video for likes and comments. Do the video to get better. Do the video to find your voice. Eventually, you will get better, and yes, the likes and comments will come, but that is a byproduct of focusing on the **process**.*

BETH GRAVES

Achievements

- Host of the top-rated podcast called *You're Not the Boss of Me*, recently listed in the top twenty-five business strategists and female empowerment coaches' category

- She mentors her team to shift their mindset, clarify their strategy, and build wildly profitable network marketing businesses (without sacrificing their sanity or souls)

- Community, consistency, and connection are her pillars for success. In under five years, Beth built a team of over 12,000 business partners and earned over two million dollars in commissions

- Beth featured in *Success From Home Magazine*, *Direct Sales Diva*, *Rise*, and *Soar Leadership Magazine* and has been a featured speaker at multiple Network Marketing industry events

- Beth lives in Wellington, FL, with her patient and handsome husband, who tolerates her singing, dreaming, and wanderlust

- She's a half-empty nest momma to two awesome humans Donny and Mackenzie

Quote:
"When we decide to collect experiences instead of things, we never run out of storage space."

- Jordan Becker

Coach's Notes:

*Beth is one of those people that everyone loves. She is a pro at making friends. I think it was about four years ago when I first got to know Beth. She was an emerging leader in her business and was so eager to keep learning. Fast forward a few years, and she attended my second ever mastermind in Sundance, Utah. At this mastermind, there were at least ten other top earners. She shared some very vulnerable stories and probably connected with more people in that mastermind than anyone there. She shared how she was a people pleaser and was awful as a leader and setting boundaries. She shared much more, which I won't go into detail about here, but the main point was that she was as real as anyone you had ever met. Being **real** is her superpower. She knows how to connect with people quickly. So, as you read this chapter, pay attention not to the realities of this incredible profession but also to Beth's unique ability to communicate with others.*

The *Real* Truth about Recruiting Your *Dream Team* (and building a *Legacy* Business)

You see the photos of the top earners on stage or in a super fancy corporate video. You hear the stories and even know the people who "made it big." On social media, it looks like every one of the top earners has a perfect office with a vision board in the background. And did they go to marketing school? Because the words they use, the stories they share are all so *perfect*.

Everyone has the same thought when they see top earners. They think, "I wonder what happens in real life?" Wonder no more. I am here to tell you exactly what the real life of a top earner looks like. I want to *really* share the happenings in the beginning, middle, and well into the journey of a top, million-dollar earner. I will share the *daily* steps you can take today to be well on your way to making a shift to the business you truly desire. I think it's important to share the perfect life and real life because I will tell you right now, they are *very* different.

There are four main steps that I took to build a successful network marketing business. These steps aren't going to blow your mind, and you may even think, "That's it?" That is because you may be over-complicating the process. Keep it simple and think about these steps. If you are not 100 percent involved in these steps, then telling you to go and do anything else won't create the results you are after.

Step 1: Believe it can be you

I know this sounds cheesy, but if your thoughts and words are not supporting the idea of "making it to the top," it isn't going to happen. Find someone who has made it that you can relate to and look to them for inspiration. Write the vision *as if* it has already happened. Visualize every single detail of you making it to a top rank in the company. Visualize it daily.

What does this look like in real life? This looks like visualizing that you're helping thousands of people when you have only enrolled one person. It's believing you are touching the lives of others while people closest to you make fun of you. It's imagining yourself paying for an all-expense trip for your family when you can barely get the necessities provided for them. You have to be willing to feel cheesy for a bit. Take video, for example, on social media. If you believe that you will get followers, customers, and team members from the videos, you show up *so differently* in that video than if you think your family is going to make fun of you and you won't sell a thing.

Believing is not easy. People always make it sound lovely, but it's hard work believing in something that you have no evidence to support. I have had countless experiences of believing in something and desperately wanting it to happen so that I didn't have to go through the humiliation of someone saying, "I told you so." Believing in yourself is a full-time job in every single step of network marketing. Even when you hit seven figures, belief doesn't stop. So, as you grow your business, always check in on your beliefs.

Step 2: Keep it simple and stay consistent

You will be tempted to think that there is a super, secret method you don't know about *yet*. Ads will pop up to assure you that you will recruit the dream team if *only* you learn this new marketing technique. While there are always new things to know and you want to be committed to growth, don't abandon the basics because they work.

The basics are simple: People need your product or business. Use the ABC method to *Always Be Connecting* with the people that need your product or company. Be willing to start conversations about your product or business. It doesn't matter if you have sold one product or one million; you always need to be connecting. This *never* stops. Someone once said to me, "It must be nice not having to recruit." But, in reality, I am *always* recruiting because I keep it simple and stay consistent.

It's all about being willing to have *the* conversation. A conversation and not a "convincersation." Shift your intention from "I am going to *get* this person" to "let's see if this is a good fit for both of us - let me share the information, ask questions and make sure this is a good fit." *You* are the CEO of your business, so who would you hire as your best. You probably wonder what I mean by this. I mean that when I thought about recruits, it was as if I was filling a position for my board of directors. I had to recruit the *right* people.

Fill your funnel with customers who *love* your products. The *best* way to recruit is to have glowing testimonials of your customer service, product results – you need to create a community around your raving customers. If you have raving fans, ask them to rave about you. Ask them to share. This is the most uncomplicated, free marketing that also converts the best.

Step 3: Build the community that supports them, and you

Get ready for real talk here. Some people create teams that are huge and amazing. You see them at your conventions or online, and you think the leader has it all figured out. But, behind closed doors, that leader is exhausted, burnt out, and maybe even a bit resentful towards their team. This is because the leader hasn't done a great job creating a community that serves their leaders, customers, and themselves. I told you I was going to be real with you!

In the beginning, all we want is people to say yes. So, we don't think about the boundaries, values, and vision that we want to create with a team. Often this leads to communities that are not precisely what that leader wants. For any of you that have teams, this may be hitting close to home for you. Let's talk about building a community. Remember step number one? If you genuinely believe you will be a leader of a team, you have to start thinking about what type of team you want to create.

You need to build a community that you want to show up in. Think about who you want to connect with and who wants to connect with you. Keep it simple. This is best done with *live* video, engaging content, and live events, zoom events. As people grow their teams, they typically start to complicate things. They think they need to reinvent the wheel to keep their customers and teams happy. This is a lie. I promise you, what built your business can sustain your business. Keep it simple and stay consistent.

I like to keep it simple and stay consistent by celebrating wins, however big or small.

No matter what, we "huddle" every week. We share gratitude, big wins, small wins, and have new and upcoming leaders take the reins on leading the huddle. This has created a community of trust and a place for people to feel supported.

A community must help bring clarity on the systems, tools, and training. One of the best ways to help foster a community of people stepping into the business and becoming leaders themselves is to bring clarity to the things you are asking them to do. Remember, keep it simple and consistent. I like to say that clarity helps you create drivers who are confident and ready to lead in their own businesses instead of you always having to be the backseat driver – this should be your goal.

Bringing clarity is the hardest part of a community. Unfortunately, most leaders learn this the hard way, which means they have people fall out of the business because they are frustrated, confused, overwhelmed, etc. My big suggestion is that you have a few simple tools with quick resources as follows:

1. Use a 14-day onboarding tool. If your company doesn't have a step-by-step training system, keep a simple Google Drive for your team. Facebook is *great*, but it isolates those who aren't group-savvy, *and* you don't own the content.

2. Provide a section in your drive that "houses" the recordings of the training sessions, curiosity post templates, and if you find a question is repeatedly asked, create a screen recording explanation.

3. Create *guides* in your Facebook customer communities that answer their frequently asked questions (How to pause an auto-ship etc.)

Instead of answering questions 24/7, direct people to the resource and always ask for three solutions before you answer (I learned this one from Rob!). This method is a *serious* game-changer. If you can create these three things, your community is going to thrive.

Remember, you are not a surgeon, so being on-call 24/7 isn't your job, and your team won't crumble. However, it will crumble if you disappear because you've become resentful of a situation you created. Clean up the pending messages during the last fifteen minutes of your work time.

And remember to direct to the resource and not be Team Google. I also love to set up an *info chat* group. This is a place where anyone that needs support or has questions can ask on the *chat*. There will always be someone to give feedback, advice, or answer questions. I let my team know that this is their best opportunity to get quick feedback, and it builds a community nicely.

You have to be willing to set your "work" hours, and once they are set, stick to them! This is where intentionally creating community is going to be huge for some leaders. When you have a community that you *love* showing up in, you pour your love and passion into them instead of being resentful that they are "taking away" from your personal life.

Step 4: Learn how to be "Just right Jackie"

Real talk, again. You are going to make a lot of mistakes in life and business. Own it and move on. You don't have to get stuck thinking you are terrible or freeze in fear because you aren't perfect. We are all made up of great and terrible things. But what we can do is work on becoming *just right*, or what I call "Just right Jackie."

Let's take social media, for example. Have you ever identified what social media personality you are? There are three types of network marketing people on social media.

1. **Spamela Pamela:** Often seen wearing a hat, t-shirt, shoes, and holding banners featuring her company name. Her friends may think she owns the company. Many of her posts offer deals, specials and ask you to join her team. Unfortunately, it feels like we are on a commercial overload, so everyone but her team turns off her channel. She gets people to join because of her constant pressure, but they don't stick around after the guilt wears off. As a result, she gets a lot of unfollows and scroll pasts.

2. **Attraction Only Amanda:** Amanda has mastered social media. She's telling unique stories, showing her personality, and providing value. We are curious about what she does because she looks like she has "something cool" going on. She waits for people to come to her because she doesn't want to be "pushy." Maybe she sounds like the perfect person you want to become on social media. Sadly, her next multi-million-dollar leader isn't the type to reach out first. Amanda loses out on the biggest leaders because they aren't the ones sitting at home consuming her content. She occasionally finds a diamond in the rough, but it only happens once. She thinks that maybe she's got some big influencer deal, but she continues to play in the minor league.

3. **Just Right Jackie:** Jackie has it *all*! She's mastered her social media content, and she isn't afraid to show off what she does in a *non-*spammy way. You will often see her sharing success videos in her stories of the dogs that use her products. She has a weekly Facebook Live show that talks all about *Using your Passion to Profit*. She knows she has a great business model and a solution for many of her followers, friends, and community. She starts conversations

and will often ask if they would like to take a look at her product. She's built trust, rapport and she's confident in her sales funnel. When she adds a new business partner, they feel confident in her simple steps to help them have their success. Jackie *knows* that her community is looking for the solutions that she offers. She's consistent. She's confident, and she's *rocking* business and life.

So how can you become your version of Jackie and make it "Just Right?" Here are a few tips:

- Create content that connects with your **ideal** audience, providing *value* (use your authentic voice)

- Focus on a connection that starts *real* conversations

- Have conversations that don't feel spammy and weird while not being afraid to offer a solution

- With community, don't be all about the number of followers you have but rather about the super fans that show up and connect with your content, stories, and live recordings

- Focus on consistency because it will compound

- Just be cool. You show up like Jackie, and you know that the world doesn't need a filter

This is *one* example of how to figure out how to be just right in your business. First, you have to decide what "just right" means for you. *Compare and Despair* is a real thing in our business. I watch people appraise themselves, their teams, and their companies because they compare themselves to others. Comparison will never be helpful for you and could create a real problem. As you build a network marketing business, you will begin to see how it feels "just right" to you. Stick with it and don't start to question "just right" because you see someone else doing it differently.

Final thoughts from Beth

Next time you're wondering what it is like to run a successful business, take a step back and ask yourself, "What will my successful business look like?" There are so many motivating people around you. Use the motivation and ditch the comparison. I have built a very successful business and life by following these four simple steps.

Don't overcomplicate things for yourself. As a bonus, I will tell you two things I do every day:

- Gratitude

I practice being *grateful* every single day! I keep a business gratitude journal, and every day since *day one*, I've written at least one thing that I am grateful for every day. I also send at least one message *every* day to one member of my team expressing my gratitude. Some days, I don't feel like it. Some days I feel like I have stepped in quicksand, and I am already up to my neck and sinking deeper. But I still find gratitude. Gratitude has helped me move on quickly and keep my business active and thriving.

- Stand by the four agreements

Every day, I stand by the four agreements that Don Miguel Ruiz created. I am impeccable with my words. I don't take anything personally, I don't make assumptions, and I always do my best.

Living by simple truths and being consistent is the key to my success, and it can help you along the journey with yours.

Coach's Notes:

Beth would always joke around that she is a hot mess and all over the place, so she had to keep everything simple. She is a master at creating simple systems for success. She does this through her simple steps, which you just read about but even more than those steps is that she is very deliberate in focusing on the most critical tasks. A great quote says, "Every master was once a disaster," and it's true! As you follow these principles to improve your current daily operation or system, focus on progress! Focus on getting a little bit better each day, week, month, quarter, and year!

GABE AND JILL PEARSON

Achievements:

- In network marketing for twelve years, full-time professionals for ten years
- Millions in monthly revenue
- Over 75,000 team members
- Our team members are in twenty-four countries and continually expanding

Jill's Quotes:

"Vulnerability is the birthplace of love, belonging, joy, courage, empathy, and creativity. It is the source of hope, empathy, accountability, and authenticity. If we want greater clarity in our purpose or deeper and more meaningful spiritual lives, vulnerability is the path."

- Brene Brown

Gabe's Quote:

"The great thief of opportunity is not failure, it's indecision."

- Jim Rohn

"A wise man investigates what fools take for granted."

- Unknown

Gabe's Story

We owned an incredible wellness company that took executive teams and slingshot them to be in the best shape of their lives in just 84 days.

We were working hard, loving our passion for helping others and raising our children, Natalie and Gabriel, who were nine and six years old. In 2009, we experienced the actual reality of The 2009 Recession - losing three six-figure contracts that were the lifeblood of our small business in 30 days.

As Divine intervention would have it, I was asked to be a keynote speaker at a Health and Fitness conference in Atlanta, Georgia. After my keynote talk, a complete stranger approached me and asked

"Have you ever heard of a particular product, and would you be willing to watch a nine-minute video on an ABC primetime investigative report?"

I looked at her, and I said, very sarcastically, "You are telling me that ABC News did a positive spin on a dietary supplement? No way! Let me see it."

Fast forward one week, we were invited to hear the whole story. Twenty-two months later, we had the choice to walk away from the fitness business and pursue this new venture full time.

Coach's Notes:

I have heard nothing but incredible things about Gabe. I have gotten to know Jill while attending the last two Masterminds. And let me tell you something, Jill has some of the most contagious positive energy I have ever seen. Every time you are around her, you come away in a good mood. Now think about this. Jill and Gabe were two people that everyone would want in their business. Yet, they had no interest for 30 years! 30 freaking years! That one lesson alone should give you hope that you never know when it will be someone's time. Don't give up on people just because they said "no" to you. The next insight is that you must be committed. As you commit, you will build credibility and confidence (assuming you are focusing on progress). Over time, not only do you become better, but the law of averages teaches us that you will find some of those other incredible leaders as you progress.

More from Gabe

Based on the studies and patents on this product, Jill and I knew we had found a new category creating science. This product was unique, and I thought the company was special.

I did extensive research before putting our name behind anything because we were concerned about our credibility. In addition, we had some reservations about the network marketing business model. We first validated the product through the National Institute of Health and Google Scholar then we checked all the boxes asking ourselves, can this company become solid and profitable?

After that extensive initial research, we were all in. We made a decision.

We were fortunate to have learned from the formulator of this product who also is known as "the father of free radical biology." I was lucky enough to have had him in Jacksonville FL as my guest. Every time we would hear his lectures and seminars, we were so excited about the possibilities of this new business. Our responsibility was to share this new science with the world.

We decided to build this business and learn to become professionals in this industry.

The first thing/activity our mentor told us to do was make a list of 100 prospects. Then he said, let's launch your business this Thursday, four days later.

Gabe: - tell the audience how you felt

I couldn't believe this individual would be willing to fly across the country and actually help me launch my business.

First, we did what we were told and launched our business the first week.

I invited forty people to a meeting in our neighborhood. Twenty-five people showed up, and sixteen enrolled within a week to 10 days.

From my experience in the fitness world, I knew I would have to call at least forty people if we wanted twenty people to show up at our first opportunity meeting. Therefore, I created urgency with my phone calls and voicemails. I would say,

"Whatever you are doing on Thursday night, cancel it!

I have something extremely exciting I want to share with you. Call me back as soon as you can!"

After this launch of our business, we went halfway up the company's compensation plan within the first month.

And we thought, wow – we got this network marketing business model down. However, we had so much more to learn about the industry and leading teams – we were literally babies in this industry - our team was small, fragile, and we had no leaders yet and our group volume did not grow for 12 months. *We had hit our first ceiling in network marketing.*

Coach's Notes:

Learn from your beginnings! Not all, but most people have more success at recruiting in month one than they do in month five. In the beginning, we have that incredible optimism and urgency. Gabe and Jill said the following, "I have something extremely exciting I want to talk to share with you. Call me back as soon as you can." They didn't know how to explain the product or the compensation plan yet. They had just started. They crushed it because they did a few things really well.

1. *They created urgency.*
2. *They kept it short.*
3. *They had high energy and boldness.*
4. *They continued to invite new people to take a look.*

All of us can learn from these principles. Go back to your first days in network marketing when you were crazy optimistic. Go back to the dreamer version of yourself and follow it with action. How many of you have been there before? Maybe you have avoided your company events, mentors, and even your own team because of the shame of not hitting a rank.

More from Gabe

That year was tough with the collapse of our small business, no cash flow and taking care of two small children.

We maintained our rank, but we did not grow.

One of our quarterly events was around the corner and I did not want to go.

Jill shared with one of our mentors that I did not want to attend our quarterly training.

I did not want to attend because it was nearly a year of being recognized at the same rank and I was embarrassed.

Our mentor said to me "If you don't attend, I will stop mentoring you." Going to company events is a non-negotiable in this industry if you want to build a solid business. "You are teaching duplication if you don't come, your team doesn't come."

Then he added, "This is an easy fix, Gabe, "Why don't you just do what you did the first thirty days of your business? Lead by example, start sharing/recruiting and enrolling again like you did the first thirty days."

He said "The speed of the group is the speed of the leader. Your team will do what you do."

We had gone into management mode without knowing we were in management mode.

I had sixteen team members doing what I was doing – managing – doing nothing.

What is management mode? Simply depending on your team to do all the recruiting. Interestingly, the minute I started to recruit, our team started to do the same. It was an eye-opening moment for me about this industry.

Breakthrough with Inviting and Enrolling

We now have a better understanding of the business. When we launched our business, we did it with a burst of activity and now fully believe this fueled our wins at the beginning of our business.

1.   Add to your database of friends, family, and business acquaintances daily. Your prospect list is the lifeblood of your business.

2.   One of our mentors said to always share your opportunity with those who you look up to professionally. That means, as a rule, we generally connect/invite prospects that have more success, more integrity, and credibility—people who are business owners to join our business.

    a.   These people have large circles of influence and credibility. In addition, they are typically open-minded and already know how to build a business.

3.   As a rule of thumb, never prejudge, assume, or make a decision for someone. We lived in a nice neighborhood and our kids went to private school; however, we had no cash flow.

4.   Never ever stop inviting and enrolling. You should always have a mindset of, "Whose life am I going to change today?"

Master the skill of the invite by keeping it simple with three steps

- Compliment

- Ask for permission

- Set the appointment

We have learned over the years when you compliment someone; their mind is open. They will listen to you. People love to hear good things about themselves, right?

We have found that if you ask for permission, for example, "Hey, are you open to learning more about this new business that we find so exciting?" people respond well. You could also say, "Are you open to looking at a side hustle with me?" or "I am launching a new business, and I'm looking for people like you - are you open to looking?"

The last step is to set the appointment after they have viewed your information. Repeat these steps over and over.

I say, "Who speaks to the most people wins."

Our next aha moment that helped to breakthrough our ceiling was after a training event. Jill and I went to the front of the room to talk to one of the speakers. He congratulated us on our success, and we explain our challenges in our business.

He asked us, "Are you in front of the room presenting?"

Gabe proudly said, "Yes! I do *all* the presentations and training."

"Now, Gabe, how many leaders on your team are presenting and training?"

"None."

He then explained how leverage can work for us in network marketing and this concept was key for us to break through to our next rank.

He said, "This business is about duplication. It's teaching people to teach people to teach people."

To grow your teams, you must leverage your business.

You must identify and teach others to present and train.

He continued, "The more teammates we had in front of the room - the more exposures of our products and opportunity the more everyone would see results. And most importantly, we would be truly leveraging our time.

As J. Paul Getty says - "I'd rather have 1 percent of the effort of 100 men, than 100 percent of my own effort."

The lightbulb went off for us and we realized this business was not about us – it was about teaching others to teach others – servant leadership at its finest.

In the words of Zig Ziglar,

"You can get everything you want in life if you just help enough other people get what they want."

Important Note

In traditional business, we were always conditioned to do everything by and for ourselves. We only knew how to use our own efforts to create our own financial success, so we always embraced the ownership mindset. However, in network marketing, in addition to taking ownership of your business (no excuses) - we must never forget this business is about others – it's about serving others.

Breakthrough with Leverage

Today we ask you, "How many people on your team do you want in front of the room?"

Leverage is everything in this business!

- Connect and identify the leaders on your teams
- Teach those leaders to present and train
- Let go and give those leaders those opportunities
- Teach those leaders to develop their leaders
- Lead by example

As we started to breakthrough by doing exactly what our mentors told us to do:

Another recruiting and enrolling burst, just like our first 30 days in our business

and continued to attend the monthly and quarterly trainings we finally started to grow again! We more than doubled our volume in 45 days, and then doubled again in 45 more days.

Those great lessons opened our eyes to the enormity of leverage, this industry and enabled us to reach the beginnings of our company's top ranks.

Breakthrough by Building Belief

Ask yourself, "Is my belief impenetrable?"

Definition of impenetrable: incapable of being penetrated or pierced

Do you fully believe? Lack of belief in the industry, your company, your product, and most importantly, yourself, will create ceilings.

Gabe on Belief

Lack of belief in yourself, the industry, your company, or product will create ceilings in your business. Lack of belief in any of these areas is a silent killer of your opportunity - your dreams.

To become impenetrable your "What and Why" must be set in stone, unshakable and unwavering.

As we launched our business my belief was bullet proof. Once I validated the product and the enormity of the opportunity no one was going to stop me from building this business. I was impenetrable. Made of Kevlar. Bullet proof. I was clear on my what and why. If someone said, "No," mentally, I politely mentally moved them out of my way and said, "Next." And I truly believed that a "No" was temporary and I would continue to follow up. Also, my what and why were clear.

What we need to be keenly aware of, if there is a shred of doubt, in yourself, the industry, your company or product, your prospects and your team will innately sniff out your lack of belief immediately, and your team will not grow to its true potential. You must be bulletproof to build this business.

Breakthrough Self-limiting Beliefs

As we continued to climb the top ranks of our company, I'll never forget, I stood in the kitchen, and Gabe was on the couch looking at his email. He says, "Jill, we just received our paycheck for this new rank."

And he excitedly tells me how much. I was excited but at the same time I

I'll never forget how I felt - like I was spinning, out of breath and full of anxiety. It was the oddest feeling.

I had never in my life earned that kind of money that was free and clear without business expenses and payroll being deducted from the bottom line.

As I reflect back now, just 26 months prior to earning that paycheck, I was struggling to buy food for our family and on this day, in my kitchen, I believe my mind was still in a place of fear and scarcity from the 2009 Recession.

In addition, the gremlins inside were chattering phrases my mom would always say, affirming lack – phrases like, are you sure ... we cannot afford ... and maybe you should not do that, Jill.

Back in my kitchen, my chest tightened, and the room spun. I become keenly aware that this negative physical reaction to our well-earned paycheck could create a ceiling in my growth as a leader, but most importantly, the growth of our team - The impact I could make in changing lives – my mission.

This immediate physical reaction was a sign an indication of self-limiting beliefs – of a scarcity or undeserving mindset. This time, I physically felt the "alarm" warning me I need to work on this belief system that no longer served me.

To Identify some of these inner beliefs try asking yourself an open-ended question.

My biggest fear of inviting is _____?

My biggest fear of being in front of the room is _____?

My biggest fear of making money is_____?

My biggest fear of leading teams is _____?

A quick and immediate response will reflect back to you almost instantly the beliefs that are working against you - that may be creating those ceilings we are working to breakthrough

Once identified we can focus on rewiring those beliefs that no longer serve us.

A mindset filled with limits will limit your business.

Tactics to rewire the belief systems that no longer serve us

Attend your companies' events – they are non-negotiable because you build belief by:

1. Connecting and learning from other leaders ahead of you - you gather golden nuggets that can change your business on a dime like ours did

2. connecting with distributors with similar rank and challenges

3. See a bigger vision

4. This is a duplication business. When you go to these events, your team will go to the events. When you do not go to trainings, your team will not go. It's as simple as that

5. Surround yourself with those who are lifting you up, encouraging, and who have had proven success in network marketing

6. You are the average of the five people you spend the most time with – Jim Rohn

7. Embrace the 3 P's

Rewind to the beginning of our network marketing journey – We were being recognized on the stage for moving halfway up the compensation plan in 30 days.

I'll never forget as Gabe and I stood on the edge of the stage right beside the black velvet curtain. "Gabe and Jill Pearson '' the announcer's voice boomed across the auditorium. I walked nervously, to the center of the stage and the bright lights pierced my eyes. The host held the mic in front of my lips and I squeaked out, I'm Jill from Jacksonville FL.

I was nervous, uncertain, and not confident. This was the beginning of my journey of believing in myself.

From there I began preparing, practicing, and presenting how to share our opportunity, to teach the basic principles of network marketing and eventually leadership talks.

By far, preparing, practicing and presenting is and will continue to grow me into the person I was designed to become.

I call this principle: The 3 P's

Prepare – outline and gather information on your topic, i.e., Invite

Practice - Practice your talk/presentation in the back yard or your porch

Present - Give yourself an audience and a deadline. Tell one of the distributors you will teach them how to invite or you will present at your next team meeting.

When you are in front of the room and you lead by example, you build your inner confidence, posture, and conviction (belief in yourself) while building belief in all areas of network marketing (industry, company, product, and most importantly ourselves).

Doctors use this principle. However they say, "See one. Do one. Teach one to build their own belief in themselves and their field of practice."

Dale Carnegie says, "When we hear the applause of the audience we develop an inner power, calm and confidence we've never experienced – the result we accomplish things we never dreamed possible."

Breakthrough by Flipping the Narrative

From our own personal ceilings, we now have Created some of our best training stories and lessons to share and most importantly we have empathy and insight with our team as they face their own breakthroughs

However, when you run up against these challenges

- Listen to mentors who have success in network marketing
- Always Invite and enroll
- Leverage your team
- Attend Events
- BELIEVE in yourself, the industry, your company and products
- Be aware and rewire the belief systems that no longer serve you

This is our first time in network marketing. We didn't, and still don't, have something magical that gives us an advantage. We simply had to believe in ourselves and what we are doing. We were coachable. If our mentors coached us, we did what they told us. We were clear where we were going, and we were consistent and blessed with incredible teams, both corporate and the field, and leaders and mentors.

Gabe's Mom, Odette, always says, "You can do anything you want to; you just have to believe you can."

Today, when I wake up, I asked myself, whose life am I going to impact today. I work to push through my personal ceilings for all of you. You drive me to act despite my fears and self-limiting beliefs. I work to rewire the belief systems that no longer serve me and focus on an even bigger purpose of impacting lives around the globe. I encourage you to do the same.

As we write these final words, we are humbled to be a part of this amazing profession, called network marketing, a solid business model that has given us so many blessings: time freedom, relationships around the world and most importantly a purpose bigger than us, of impacting lives. Now we invite you, today to be the exception and Connect and Make an Impact around the world.

Coach's Notes:

Despite all of Gabe and Jill's success, they still shared the struggles they had. They still felt embarrassed. They still doubted themselves. They still wanted to avoid going to a big event because their business was going backward. If you are struggling, you are normal. The key is what you are going to do! It starts with your mindset, and then that good mindset leads to taking massive action. It isn't going to happen overnight, but nothing worthwhile ever does. You are worth it! Let's make it happen.

JACKIE WILSON

Achievements:

- Opened the Canadian market for her company
- First to reach the top of the compensation plan and earn 6+ figures in Canada for her company
- Highly sought-after motivational speaker and mentor

Quote:

"If You Believe It, You Will Achieve It!"

All fun and games until you're desperate

I think we can all remember the excitement we felt starting our first network marketing business. I can remember it like it was yesterday! I was in my early twenties and a friend had received her products to get started in a cosmetics company. We were looking at everything together and it felt like possibility and success were all sitting there right on her kitchen table. She was going to have parties, sell products, and make a ton of money. It sounded like the perfect gig and I wanted it.

I had no idea about network marketing whatsoever. No one in my family had ever been involved in it, and I knew nothing about what it meant to be involved, but my friend was doing it, and that's all I needed to say "yes." I signed up, got my products, and then failed miserably.

Does this sound like a familiar story to any of you? It was a complete and utter failure, and to be honest, I didn't take any of it seriously. I didn't do the training and I didn't hold myself accountable. For me, network marketing was a way to be with my friends and it looked like fun. I didn't consider that network marketing was a viable option for anything other than a reason to throw parties and hang out with friends. I honestly didn't care about the company or the product, and when my friend quit, I quit. It was as simple as that.

This pattern of joining a company and quitting continued to happen over the years. I would beg people to host parties, and if I made any money at all, it would be just enough to cover my product. I didn't make any money and only did it for fun and never to have an actual successful business. I came from a family where my dad worked at the same job for over thirty years. I thought that was what success was.

I thought you got hired at a job, were given a certain amount of money for the job you did, given a certain amount of time off for yearly vacation and you were expected to be there for a set number of hours a day. You lived your life by those means. The money you made at your job determined the kind of life and lifestyle you could lead. I thought success came in the form of having money left over after you paid your bills. Other than that, I never dreamt of anything further.

After years of turning and burning in various companies, I began to doubt the entire network marketing profession, believing that those successful people whose names were in the limelight were merely better than me. Life went on, and I periodically questioned the validity of network marketing, which often came after I burnt through yet another opportunity. I went on to get married, got divorced, got married again, had kids, and switched careers twice. However, I was still never able to find success in network marketing or even in my regular 9-5 job. Something was missing for me, but I had no idea what.

One day while I was thinking about this, I decided that other people could succeed in network marketing because they won some kind of network marketing lottery. They surely had mentors who cared about them; they must have had better products; they were lucky enough to be on outstanding teams, or they had friends and family who all loved buying from and supporting them. I also believed that they had success because they were more attractive and better looking than me (I actually believed this!). They were well put together, appeared to come from money or were in a different and higher class than me altogether. So, I convinced myself that they had things that I didn't have and would never have, therefore, success in network marketing was not reserved for "regular people" like me.

Looking back on it all now, I was what I like to call a "network marketing tourist." I liked the idea of the profession but didn't take it seriously and I didn't believe I would have the same great success that others had. The truth be told, I never attended events, I didn't train or learn the skills needed even to have success, albeit I had never had anyone help me learn them either. I honestly thought you got the kit of products; you called your family and friends, begged them to have parties and buy from you, and when they didn't, or you burned through everyone you knew, it was game over. My friends would reluctantly host parties for me, and I prayed that guests at those parties would book a party so my business could continue.

If they didn't, and when the well ran dry, my new business was over. Therefore, in my mind, those who had success in the profession had more friends and support than I did. I also admit that I was terrible at presenting at parties. How could I be good at something when I didn't bother to do the training? I didn't stand a chance.

Mind monster stops many of us

The day finally came when I was able to answer my own question about the problems of being involved in network marketing. I was the reason I was unsuccessful, and the profession wasn't to blame for my lack of success. My *mind monster* had always come and swallowed me whole every time I started in a new company. I would let the negativity and comments from those around me prevent me from moving ahead. I let my fears, doubts, and insecurities get in my way. I cared more about what others thought about my choice to be involved in the profession than the reason why I was doing it. I would downplay the profession and what it offered because I didn't take any of it seriously, and I also allowed the negative comments that my family and friends made about it hold me back.

I didn't believe that network marketing was, in actuality, a true profession. When I was able to see all the ways that I was holding myself back, and I decided to go all in and become a student of the profession and put my goals and dreams first, it became incredibly freeing. It was a total "a ha" moment! When I focused on outside things like the mentors that other people had that I didn't, their seemingly more significant networks, the achievements of others (and lack of my own), I realized I was focusing on all the wrong things. I decided that I would stay in my lane, keep my head down and work on myself and my own business. I wasn't going to focus on anyone but me, and I reminded myself that what others were doing and what they had/didn't have was none of my business. Instead of focusing on what I couldn't change, I started to focus on myself, which I could change!

Part of taming the *mind monster* is being rock-solid in knowing why you started your business, what you want from it and what the consequences will be of not working hard to accomplish your goals. It's also knowing what you love and don't love about yourself and your life, knowing what you want and don't want, and being open to discovering who you genuinely are regardless of what others may think or say. This mindset helps you focus on what gets you excited and keeps you staying on the path of your "why."

I approach every day as if I've been handed "life's daily menu." Think about it like this, you get to choose which side of the menu you wish to order from every single day. One side of the menu says, "You're going to have a terrific, happy, enjoyable, productive day." The other side of the menu says, "You're going to be uptight. It's going to be a stressful day and you will be frustrated and negative." So, before you even begin your day, choose which side of the menu you're going to live by. Happiness and love are a choice. Frustration and negativity are a choice, too.

How you respond to the situations in your life is a choice. How you think, respond or react (or don't respond or react) is a choice. Just like being negative is a choice. How you approach your business is a choice. You can choose to show up spectacularly in your business every single day, or you can decide to be negative and not show up at all. You get to choose every single day, so my friend, choose wisely.

I have been with my current company for over six years. I was one of the first people to open our company in Canada. I was also the first person to make six figures in the company in the Canadian market. None of this ever would have happened if I didn't tame my *mind monster*, and trust me, my *mind monsters* were big ones! Opening up a company in another country is no walk-in-the-park! There were tremendous obstacles and adversities to overcome, and there were many (many!) potholes, twists, and turns in the journey.

Unfortunately, too many people decide to turn a pothole they encounter on their journey into a stop sign. So, whenever I encounter an obstacle in the road, I go to work and figure out a way around it. It's not always easy to do, but I've learned that when your *why* is bigger than the obstacle, you'll crush it. Trust me. It doesn't stand a chance of holding you back!

> **Coach's Notes:**
>
> *One thing that has stood out to me about Jackie is that she is one of the best learners I have ever met despite her success. She is still a student, always studying the latest books and most updated training. But even more important is that she takes action upon learning. The ability to learn how to learn is the greatest ability one can have. Jackie possesses this unique ability.*

No one is going to save us

Before I started with my current company, we were in a dire situation as a family. My husband was having major health issues that were very serious and prevented him from working. I lost job after job and just couldn't find my footing. We were barely keeping the lights on and the roof over our heads. We had no money and I felt utterly helpless. Our lives had spiraled out of control, and I felt like I couldn't do anything about it. Everywhere I turned for help, I had door after door slammed in my face. I didn't know what was going to happen or how we were ever going to get our lives turned around.

I remember one night so vividly. I had put on a Disney movie for my kids and fed them microwave popcorn and Kool-Aid for dinner because that was the only food we had in the house. I fell to my knees that night and I prayed that I would receive the strength I needed to stand up, shake myself off and go and make a life for my family and me. I was praying for a miracle. I realized that the way out of our situation wasn't going to be easy, but I was not put on this earth to suffer. My mama didn't raise me to be weak! I was more determined than ever to stop being a victim and start being victorious in my life. Then, a few days later, a friend reached out to me with a new network marketing opportunity. I knew that if I was going to get my family out of our situation, I would have to do something entirely different from what I had been doing up to that point.

I knew that no one was going to come and save us; it was going to be up to me. I grabbed a hold of the opportunity and haven't looked back since. I am happy to report that today, my husband is healthy, and because of my hard work and resilience, we are beyond blessed to have the freedom to make choices and live the lifestyle we have always wanted and on our terms. During our struggle, every door was closed for us, so I worked hard and built my own damn door. I might have been down, but I sure as heck wasn't out! If anyone counted me out, that was a big mistake! I was tough, resilient, and not going to let anyone or anything hold me back from living the life that I dreamt of living.

I share this with you because we all face adversity. We are more powerful than we give ourselves credit for – I genuinely believe this. We can change our circumstances if we believe in ourselves for a moment and make the courageous decision to do whatever it takes to make change happen. You either let life happen to you or you make life happen for you. Once you've made the decision, you cannot and will not be stopped.

The *real* reason for your *why*

You have likely heard the saying in network marketing that "*your why should make you cry.*" I have watched people literally roll their eyes when they hear this, but I think it is because they don't truly understand the concept behind it. When you are desperate enough, you will do whatever it takes to change your circumstances. My "why" for doing this business made me cry, and it still does today. I started my business because I was desperate. I could not afford to fail one more time and my family needed me more than ever. From the day I started my business, I approached it with a *"failure is not an option"* mindset. Too many people make their businesses optional. If you do that, you most certainly will not find the success you are looking for.

A few years ago, I started working with an excited new distributor on my team. She brought so much life and fun to our team and told me all about herself during one of our initial telephone discussions. When I asked her why she was in network marketing, her answer was the typical, "to make more money." When I pressed her to elaborate further, she wasn't able to answer me and quickly changed the subject. As the months went by, I watched as she flipped and flopped her way along; some months were decent and left her excited, while others left her deflated and questioning her own abilities.

Sadly, the latter was what I witnessed with her more often than not, and she eventually went silent. She stopped showing up on our calls and for training and her numbers steadily declined. When asked what was going on or if she needed any help, she would always say how busy she and her life were, etc. Finally, after a few months, we scheduled a Zoom meeting as I wanted to be face-to-face with her. We exchanged the usual pleasantries, and then I decided to face the elephant in the room. I asked her what was really going on. As our discussion progressed, I pressed her about what she ultimately wanted from the network marketing profession, even if it meant not being in our company. I kept peeling back the many layers of answers she was providing. Suddenly, she lowered her head and began to cry. We had discovered why she was in the profession and what would happen for her life if she didn't reach her goals. She was so overcome with emotion that it took her a few minutes to pull herself together.

I immediately cheered for her and told her that this was her new starting point! This point was where she was going to work every single day! I had her write it down and post it everywhere in her home. She even had it on a sticky note in her car and as the wallpaper on her phone. She kept it front and center as a reminder every single day. She shared that she had never had anyone believe in her. Instead, she had people who mocked her for doing network marketing and who were really negative. This bad treatment caused her to withdraw from continuing as it was too stressful and painful for her.

She would self-sabotage wins because she had no one around her that believed in her and no one in her circle cared. She felt defeated by this. I asked her if her dreams and her goals meant more to her than those who belittled her. She wholeheartedly said they did, and with her enthusiastic permission, we started to change her mindset. I sent her books, podcasts and a gratitude journal. She began to break free from the mental chains that had been holding her hostage for more years than she cared to admit. She threw herself into her business and with the team because it was where she felt the most love and support.

Today, she is consistently working her business and having steady success. She is now able to help others who she sees struggling just like she was. This is proof that fear and limiting beliefs are not permanent. Finding the right mentor, working consistently on your personal growth and development daily, and surrounding yourself with the right people are key to making meaningful strides forward in your business.

Coach's Notes:

Good leaders have vision, while great leaders give vision. One of the hardest parts about becoming a leader inside of network marketing is having those tough conversations. Jackie did so in a way that illustrates authentic leadership. First, she knew she needed to have a challenging conversation. Second, she knew that she first needed to convey her intent so that she didn't come across as a boss or manager but like a leader, instead. Third, she listened. Fourth, after all of that, she cast a vision of hope and optimism. No, not one of those fake visions where you tell them what they want to hear but a true vision of possibility. Fifth, Jackie then broke it down into simple steps to help this team member. These are five simple steps to help you increase duplication quickly within your teams.

Patience is a virtue

Another area where people get stuck is that they lack the patience to build a successful network marketing business. We are becoming more and more fixated on instant gratification. We want everything instantly and we want success immediately. If we aren't "rich" by the end of the first few months, we quit and move on to the next shiny opportunity. We quit before we ever have a chance of finding our stride or learning the skills required to build a successful business.

We quit before we give ourselves a real chance and we lack the patience to learn and grow. It baffles me that some people will spend years working in the same job, getting small raises here and there (if they are lucky), grinding it out day after day in jobs they don't necessarily like and are living pay-cheque-to-pay-cheque, never getting ahead. Still, if they don't see immediate success in network marketing, they're out and then blame the profession or the company. Why will they afford their 9-5 job time but won't afford their "Plan B" / side gig at the same time?

Building a business and changing your life takes time. We need to be honest with ourselves and face the fact that we aren't going to see success quickly and network marketing isn't a get-rich-quick scheme. Trust me, if anyone tells you otherwise, run! When you start to build your business, you have to remind yourself that you aren't going to be an overnight success and that it's normal and acceptable for it to take months and even years to happen. Success will come at the right time and after you've been consistent in your business efforts. So, keep chipping away and keep working at it. It can be hard to afford yourself the time and patience when you're in a desperate situation or circumstance, I get it. This is one reason that working on your *why* and keeping it front and center at all times is so vitally important.

My family's lives relied entirely upon every single effort that I made. Every single day they were reliant on the actions I took in my business. I went into this business with a deeply rooted *why* that still makes me emotional. I want you to think about your why. Why are you doing this business? Why are you investing in yourself? Why does any of this matter to you? What are the consequences for your future if you don't stick it out and work hard to make your goals a reality?

You have to know your deep-rooted why and make sure that it stirs an emotion in you. When you reach the place in your heart that inspires your reason to build a business and the outcome makes you emotional, work from that place every single day. It has to be as important to you as breathing. Remember how I started in network marketing? Because it looked like fun, it was a reason to throw parties and hang out with friends. Unfortunately, that was *not* enough for me to work hard or keep me motivated to continue. Be honest with yourself and look at why you started your business and why you need it. Is your reason enough to push through the hard times and obstacles? If the honest answer is "no," it's time to dig deeper and find the *reason* that is rooted deep inside of you. If the reason why you're here is superficial and not important enough to you, you will make excuses and won't put in the required work, period. You won't show up in your business and you will most certainly spin your wheels as I did for so many years.

I was raised by parents who supported my endeavors. Anything that my brother and I would undertake, our parents were always encouraging. They encouraged us to go all in and to do everything to the best of our abilities. Our thoughts were, "If you're going to do it, do it well." My mom, in particular, raised us in an environment that cultivated a strong sense of self-image and self-esteem. Every time my brother and I would leave the house, my mom would stop us briefly and say, "remember who you are." It was a reminder for us to maintain our core values and provided us with a strong sense of self-image and self-esteem.

Self-esteem and self-image

Your self-esteem and your self-image are two different things. Your self-esteem is the value you place on yourself, and your self-image is how you see yourself. So, ask yourself some questions and answer them honestly, even if the answer hurts you to admit. Do you see yourself as capable or incapable? Do you see yourself as deserving or undeserving? Do you see yourself as good or bad? Do you see yourself as attractive or unattractive? Do you see yourself as successful or unsuccessful? Do you see yourself as worthy or unworthy? How you see yourself matters. If you answer these questions about yourself negatively, you are putting yourself into boxes that are limiting you from your true potential. You are holding yourself back, because everything possible in your life is on the outside of those limiting boxes. You have to expand the way you see yourself!

We must learn to tame the *mind monster*, especially in business, because there will be many ups and many downs. One way of doing this is learning to let go of our misguided perceptions of ourselves and not caring about what other people have said (or say) about us. If part of your problem is that you're holding on to the past, remember that the past is behind you for a reason. Leave it there and know you are starting a new chapter in your journey. We have to open up the possibility of becoming somebody new and claiming a new sense of self-worth and self-esteem. We have to be willing to face the mind monster and say, "I'm no longer going to look at myself this way. I'm going to choose to look at myself as the person I want to become." We have to learn how to tell our *mind monsters* to stop talking and take a seat! *You* own your thoughts, and *you* control them. Your *mind monster* doesn't. It's time to tell that beast to take a hike! My mother once said that we write our life stories and never hand the pen to someone else to write it. Want to know what's really cool about that? We can rewrite our stories over and over again as many times as we want, so today, I'm encouraging you to pick up the pen and start to write the story you were born to create.

Another area that causes people to struggle is that they treat their business like a hobby. If you are going to treat it like a hobby, it will cost you like a hobby. All hobbies cost money. Suppose you are making wreaths, for example. You have to buy all the material (which can be quite costly) and then spend time making the wreath. Rarely do we ever get paid for our hobbies, and if we do, we never recoup money for the time we've put into it or the initial cost of the materials. Hobbies cost money; businesses make you money. This is a great way to check yourself and see if you are treating this as an actual business or if you are a hobbyist.

Stop fearing and start believing

So often the *mind monster* is being driven by one emotion: fear. To have a life you have never had before, you have to do things you have never done before. This leads people down the path of fear. They start to doubt themselves. They are afraid to step outside the norm of what they've always known – their comfort zone. We are scared of what other people will think and are fearful of rejection. We are scared of offending, or we are afraid of being offended ourselves. We are afraid of failing, and alternatively, we can also be frightened of having success. We are worried that if we succeed people will look at us differently.

We are afraid of being in the spotlight or being seen as a leader. We want to know the outcome before it comes, and if we can't see it, we fear that it may never come, or we fear what might come along the way. We don't know if we will be able to handle it, so we do what we've always done; we play it safe. We don't stretch ourselves. We don't want to fail. We don't want rejection. We are afraid of being hurt. We don't want what we don't know unless we are sure of the result, so we settle. We let life happen to us and we merely survive instead of thriving.

Fear is the underlying reason why people get held back in network marketing. Fear is what drives our *mind monster* to take over and keep us stuck where we are. One of the tactics of the *mind monster* is to use fear to keep us stuck. If we stay stuck, we aren't allowed to dream, and we start to believe that certain lifestyles and experiences aren't for people like us. We lie to ourselves to comfort ourselves instead of throwing caution to the wind and leaping into life. This thinking is how so many people get and stay stuck. They won't afford themselves the right to go after their dreams.

We all come into this profession with limiting beliefs. We wear them around like labels; "Hi, my name is _____ I'm not smart enough" or

"I'm not worthy," etc. But I know from experience that you don't have to keep any label that isn't serving you and most of the labels we are wearing are flat out lies. You really can become anything you want to become. Trust me, who I am today is not the person I was over six years ago when I started my business, thank God!

When we come into network marketing and start our businesses, we still have limiting beliefs whether we admit it or not. We don't honestly believe that we can have success because we don't know what success feels like. We almost dip a toe or crawl into the business. On some level, we truly don't think that we are even worthy of having success. We hope for the best, but we don't believe that success is for us, and we tell ourselves that it's reserved for other people.

We don't believe in ourselves enough to have and be all those wonderful things that we see others having and doing. We don't believe in our abilities. We are so limited by the little voice inside our heads, which has been there for years, that tells us that we *can't be* and *can't do* and *aren't good enough*. Most of this comes from the likelihood that we have never had anyone believe in us or encourage us before. Therefore, we don't know what it feels like to have that level of belief. Maybe you're like me and somewhere along the way in your life you had people actually strip you of any self-worth; therefore, you can't see yourself as being successful or living the life you truly dream of living. It is vitally important that you work on your mindset, that you work on your personal growth and development, and that you permit yourself for the first time in your life to dream.

But not just dream - put a plan in place to make it happen. Surround yourself with people who inspire you, who uplift you and who breathe life into you. We need to stop being around negative uninspiring people who take us away from success and tear us down. This can be hard to do because often it comes from those closest to you. Limiting your exposure to these kinds of people when at all possible will be extremely helpful for you. You also need to shed the layers of the limiting beliefs that you've worn for so long and slay the *mind monster* that has been holding you back. Take off that limiting name tag that you've been wearing for far too long and write a new one that shows just how fabulous you are. Remember, it's YOUR life and YOU get to decide how it plays out.

I encourage you today to discover why you desire to have a successful network marketing business. What means enough to you to inspire you to show up in your business every day? Then, consider what would happen in your life if you don't! Will you be able to live the life you dream of living? Will you be able to change your circumstances? Will you get out of debt? Will you be able to retire? I encourage you to become a student of the profession and decide to go all in to learn and grow. On days when you're struggling, ask yourself this question, "How would the person I'd like to become do the thing(s) I'm about to do?" Think that over for a moment and then get to work, working as if you are already the person you are striving to be.

Today, I hereby permit you to issue your *mind monster* an eviction notice. My dear reader, you are a strong, badass CEO, which stands for "Crushes Every Obstacle!" You've got this, now slay the day!

Coach's Notes:

Mindset will eat skills and systems for breakfast. Jackie has lived this and taught this to thousands. No matter how many skills you learn, none of them will matter unless you master your mindset, a constant journey. I still strive for one hour of personal development every day because I need that continuous nourishment. Create a bare minimum that you will commit to every day in your personal development journey. Then, stick to it. Over time, those small steps will lead to incredible accomplishments.

JENIFER MCCANN

Achievements:

- Hit top rank in her current company in eight months
- Has earned five incentive trips in networking marketing and counting
- Top thirteen team in the company for the past three years in her current company
- Seven-figure earner
- Number three in the company for promoting new leaders within their first year in the company

Quote:

**"Make your vision so clear that
your fears become irrelevant."**

- Kerwin Rae

Make a bold statement that is time-sensitive

I have had great success with my network marketing business. But this type of success didn't come with my first try in network marketing. I spent many hours thinking about what made this time around different. Of course, there is something about finding the right company with the right people. But there was something else that was even more important. When I started with the other companies, I started with the same mindset. I would say to myself, "Let's just see where this goes. I have nothing to lose."

I would start sharing with my friends and family, but I wouldn't engage in training and personal development because it wasn't serious to me. I was "seeing where this went." Anything that I gained from those companies was better than what I set myself up for because I had set myself up for nothing!

One of the keys to building a successful network marketing business is being intentional in your thinking. If you have the "let's see where this goes" mindset, you are setting yourself up to fail. This mindset shifts the responsibility from you and sets you up for something that will not work out. I see this in businesses, friendships, and marriages. This mindset never leads to success. When you have no vision, you have no purpose.

With my current company, I knew before I even started that my mindset needed to change. I knew I was responsible for my attitude and thoughts about the business. So, I shifted my perspective and decided to do the personal development work intentionally. When I signed up, I told my sponsor, "I hope you're ready. We are going to build an empire." From that first bold statement came pressure and accountability on me to back it up. I was taking ownership and stepping into my role. It was up to me to do the work needed to make that statement true.

You can't say out loud that you're going to build an empire and then just coast slowly into it and take minimal risks. If you make that bold, scary declaration, your mind will begin to find ways to get you there with laser focus and direction. Once I learned about the ranks my current company offered, I made an even bolder and more realistic statement. I said I wanted to reach the top of the company in less than one year. What I was doing was taking my first bold statement and creating detail around it. I was adding layers of accountability. This is how mindset works. You can make a bold statement about building an empire, but you have to get detailed about it. How are you going to do it, and how long is it going to take you? What are you willing to do to make that happen? Without having this clarity of vision, I would likely still be a stressed-out teacher trying to find a way to make it through each day without losing my mind!

Adding that time element and specific rank turned my vision from a vague dream into a much more concrete goal that I could break down into smaller steps. Your big dreams don't just happen. They are achieved through small actionable steps every single day. If you want to achieve that bigger goal like I did, you have to give yourself small steps to work on.

I wrote my vision statement on my large dry erase board to see it every single day. There were obstacles and times that I felt the business was slowing down, but it didn't matter. I had my focus and mindset right in front of me. I hit that rank within eight months! I kept my mindset laser-focused on being at the top of the company with my empire realized in less than a year. Mindset matters! What you focus on will grow. If you focus on failure, your failure will grow. If you focus on the future and your big dream, it will grow!

Coach's Notes:

*The world **loves boldness**. It makes people curious, and it is contagious. As the quote goes, "fortune favors the bold." Jenifer was very intentional with precisely what she wanted. As Jenifer mentions, boldness creates pressure. You need to shift your perspective on mindset. Billie Jean King said, "pressure is a privilege." She said that because when there is pressure, it implies something is meaningful. You want that pressure and accountability. If you're going to stop playing small and get unstuck, it starts with **boldly declaring** what you will do, but of course, it doesn't stop there.*

Share your vision with others

Part of mindset and vision is accountability, like I talked about before. You must be accountable to yourself and others. I suggest having at least one to two people with whom you can share your vision fearlessly. The more you express your goals for your business and life, the more focused you are on moving in that direction.

For me, my husband was always the first person I shared things fearlessly with. Every night we have "date night," where we get rid of all distractions and just talk or watch tv. Many nights at the beginning of this business, our talks were of our dreams. We got specific about the income we wanted to earn, what we would do with the money, and what steps we needed to get there. Then, we would talk about our key players and how they fit into that vision and help them achieve their own. It enabled him to dream and plan realistic and actionable ways to make those dreams a reality.

The second person that I always share my vision with is my sponsor. From day one, having a like-minded person was critical to bounce ideas off of and brainstorm together the things that we felt were needed to achieve the ultimate vision of our team. I feel like this was also a fundamental difference for me. We knew what we wanted for our team, down to the culture, the opportunities, and how it would be connected. Once we knew that, we had to go and make it happen. It helped to have someone that held me accountable through weekly calls and daily check-in conversations.

In the beginning, it can be scary to open up to someone about how you envision your business with specifics, especially if it isn't necessarily the same as what everyone else is going for. However, our minds are powerful, and when you have someone in your corner who knows what your intentions are, they can better give you the feedback you need to get yourself back into place when things get tough, and you feel like giving up. Many times over the past few years, I've been guilty of having a fear mindset. My sponsor kindly says the same phrase every time, "Go ahead and vent to me, but then we need to pivot." And then, she lists all the things we have accomplished that have been spot on with the vision we dreamt of in the beginning.

Journaling-track your wins!

Another huge key to bringing your vision into your business is journaling. Journaling is something that nearly every personal development book tells us to do. I'm not really someone who is into journaling about my feelings, so I never paid much attention to this. I found it too "fluffy" because I had to work on my business and goals. If you're like me, I have good news for you! Journaling doesn't have to be fluffy.

I've found success in journaling differently when I need to readjust my plans in business to plan for my next goal. Track your wins! Every day we have wins in this business. They may be personal wins or things that we had a part in for our teammates. Either way, I would stop at the end of each day and write down three wins I had for the business and three wins I had personally that day.

Choosing to focus on these positive accomplishments wraps your day up on a positive note. So many days are busy, and we feel like we didn't accomplish anything. Or our team is having a slow month, and we feel like it is all falling apart. We continue on that positive path by intentionally writing down the good things that we could do that made a positive impact. It is so much easier to take a risk and do something outside your comfort zone when you're feeling good about things. This is a way to ensure your mindset is always positive and focused on your ultimate vision. It helps you understand that roadblocks outside our control may happen, but that doesn't mean everything will derail. It transforms your mindset from a fear mindset to a growth and gratitude mindset, where you appreciate all the wins you and your team are experiencing. You can also focus on changing course when things aren't going as you initially planned.

Coach's Notes:

"A goal unwritten is merely a wish." Author Unknown. Can you imagine having this huge life-changing goal and not telling anyone about it? Can you imagine having no accountability for this huge goal and only keeping it to yourself. Yes, telling others is scary and bold, but it is an absolute must. Jenifer knew that if she wanted to build an empire, she needed to share her goals publicly. She also knew she needed that accountability and tracking. The NCIS studied accountability and found that you can have up to 96 percent more success when you have an accountability partner. Deep down, we all know this. This goes for everything from working out at the gym to achieve anything worthwhile.

Casting vision into your team

Your vision isn't just for you. At some point, you will want to share it with your team because it involves them, too. This is my favorite part of having a team. There is nothing else in the world like having a role in someone's dream; in helping to show a person their true capability. I was worried that when I stopped teaching after 12 years, I would miss this part of my passion. But, as a teacher, seeing that lightbulb moment was something I craved daily. I wasn't the teacher behind the desk. I was the one crouched down beside a student's desk, talking them through a problem and asking all the questions. When they would light up all at

6 FIGURES AND BEYOND

once when they had a breakthrough and exclaimed "OH!" or "I get it now!" Those were the moments that made it worthwhile.

In network marketing, we can have that same impact, which keeps us going and gives us that internal motivation to keep pushing through and doing the work. We can't sit behind our computer and watch the numbers for this to happen. We have to "crouch down by the student's desks," and work through this business hand-in-hand and help our organizations see their potential and realize the opportunities in front of them. One of the first ways to do this is through coaching calls.

In coaching conversations, ask good questions that allow conversations. Don't just hop on the call and start telling the person what to do. That can be overwhelming and may give them actual steps to solve one problem, but it won't help them with their vision, which is more critical to their success. Instead, ask questions such as "what is something you feel good about with your business in the last week?" When they tell you, ask them to walk you through how it happened. Get excited with them! This excitement will help them grab that momentum and desire to keep taking steps forward.

The first time you talk to each person, ask them what their vision for their business is. They may not know immediately. Help them by talking about why they signed up and what this business will do for them. This helps them start the vision creation process. Then, you can ask what one goal they have for the week, or whatever period you have between your calls, and how that will be a step towards that ultimate vision.

Always pump them up with an affirming statement at the end of the call, like "I know you can do this! I can't wait to hear when you book those three new parties or reach out to those five new leads." You'll learn so much about a person when you have these calls. It will help ensure that you are helping them with their vision, not just the one you have for them. Create records of each of these calls so that when you follow up, you are focused on what goals you set on the previous calls, and you can keep tracking forwards towards reaching them.

Vision boarding is another excellent tool for getting people to see how the business fits into their overall goals in life. These are fun to do both virtually and in person. If you have a local team, getting them together to craft actual vision boards can be a great team-building activity. Begin with some background about the purpose of a vision board and what kinds of things they should put on it. Remind them that some goals may be easier to achieve, and some may be so scary they contemplate not even putting them on the board.

The magic is in having them out in the open, so their mind focuses on how to get there. Have supplies on hand for these, such as magazines, crafting supplies, markers, etc. Virtual vision boards or even just statements for those that don't love to participate in the visual part are a great way to involve those that aren't local or reach more people at once. Make this an engaging experience where people can be vulnerable and converse as they create their visions. If a teammate prefers to do it on his own, try and have him share with you (or his own sponsor/upline) so that at least it is still out there in the universe, and they can be cheered on.

Helping other people meet their goals on your team is helping them, but it is also helping you move towards your vision for your business. It is so empowering to me to see that we can help ourselves by helping others.

This part is something with which many people struggle. As we help others go after their goals and dreams, we also have to give teammates opportunities to create things and possibly even fail. For example, if someone is terrific at fielding objections, ask them to do a live video and share their experiences. Don't worry about whether they give all the correct answers or do a perfect job speaking. The more critical factor is that they're recognized and given a chance to share, which boosts motivation and confirms they are on the right track. We want the right actions to become the right habits.

Failure is an opportunity to learn. The more you don't make a big deal about it and help your team move forward, the more they will adopt this mindset. They start to see in themselves what you see in them. One easy way to do this is to have a spotlight feature on your team. You can choose the timeline, but once every (week, month, etc.) choose a teammate to share their experience and journey. They will be flattered, but also, they will think critically about the positive things they have to share. Focusing on those positive experiences will keep them focused on what more they can do to reach their goals.

A gal on my team mentioned once that it was on her bucket list or vision board to train the entire company on a field training call. Our company has an invitation procedure, where they call you up and ask you if you'll present for our training days once per week. This particular lady was fantastic at what she does, and I truly felt like it would do so much for her in her business to check this off. So, I called the home office and gave them her name.

They called her up a couple of weeks later, and she was elated! She couldn't believe that she was worthy, which one would think she would have known the whole time since she frequently tops the charts and earns all company incentives. But for her, this empowerment was what she needed. Not only did she slay the training for the company, I saw a change in her business and leadership. She began planning more intentionally and working to empower those on her own team. You may not be able to call the home office of your company but think about what you can do to help your downline realize its potential and light that fire that may be dwindling.

Another way to empower your team to see the vision tangibly is to create systems that make it easy to follow. For example, I worked on Daily Method of Operation (DMO) checklists with my business partner that we passed along to our team. On these checklists were tangible action items that every person on the team could do in less than 30 minutes per day to help them see their vision come to life by being consistent daily.

We pulled apart the week into daily chunks. Some items on the list were repeated daily, such as connecting with five new people - other items varied by day, such as a daily IPA that works for our specific business or what type of content to post on social media platforms. These checklists were built for the inexperienced network marketer to help them see the steps leading them to their ultimate vision. A tangible way to put what may seem abstract and "dreamy" at first into actionable items that will work!

Speak those strong statements to your team

I'll never forget one of the first significant conversations with one of my top leaders. I asked her what she wanted to do with the money she made from this business, and she replied that she wanted to buy a particular mop. A mop! It was maybe $250. I saw *so* much potential in this gal that it shocked me that she would only have a goal of $250 in a month. My response was, "Think bigger. *Way* bigger. What would your ultimate goal be because you're going to make it *big* in this company!" This time, she said that she would love to be able to pay her husband's car payment or, someday, the mortgage. For her, staying home with their two young children while her husband pursued his military career had left her feeling helpless and guilty. She wanted to be a significant contributor again.

I'll never forget two short months later when she left me a voice text through tears, telling me that she just paid her mortgage that month in full. Or a few months later, when she said she paid off her husband's car! That conversation was pivotal not only in our relationship but also in her career. She needed a push to dream big. She needed someone to tell her they believed in her and that she would do big things here. Of course, it is much different from having those scary thoughts yourself, but for someone else to notice it in you is *huge*. Oh, and she did end up getting herself that mop!

You have to care about other people's dreams. You have to believe that they can make anything happen. I learned this technique from our company's top earner. When I was just a few *weeks* into my business, she called me on the phone.

First of all, I was in disbelief that she would have even noticed me on her team. I was at a level so far down she didn't even get paid for me. But she talked to me on the phone and told me how much she saw in me. She asked those good questions. She wanted me to pinpoint how much money I wanted to make and what level I wanted to reach. I had already said I wanted to build an empire, but to have someone else tell me that they believed it was everything. I didn't want to let myself down, but I sure as hell didn't want to let her down! I've kept that conversation in my heart for almost four years. When I doubt my path or contributions to this business, I think back and know that I must have shown something special. You have got to have the conversations. *Tell* those that you see as runners what you see in them. It will light a fire faster than any match you could otherwise use.

Your mindset matters. You are absolutely in charge of creating whatever you want in this life. It isn't always easy, but it is so worth it. You don't have to settle your dreams at a mop. You can dream big and then go out, hold yourself accountable, and take action to make it happen.

Coach's Notes:

Good leaders have a vision, but great leaders give vision. Good leaders are committed. Good leaders know they will not quit. While that is an incredible start, it isn't good enough. Great leaders build empires. Great leaders empower others. Great leaders give vision. Jenifer isn't just telling you what to do based on hearsay. She is telling you based on experience. Everyone is looking for the secret sauce tips, but they don't stop to implement them when they hear them. Take the time to implement this incredible chapter, and let's have you become the **boldest** *version of yourself!*

JENNIFER STROMAN

Achievements:

- Founder of Sparkle+Roots and corporate sponsor leader
- Small town Texas girl, girl mom, soon-to-be grandma, and cat lover
- Six-figure earner and top leader of her company
- Been in the industry for over twenty years
- Leads a multimillion-dollar team consisting of thousands on a mission to empower women
- Helped multiple women achieve six figures, and thousands earn a monthly "comma" check
- Featured speaker for multiple years at her company conventions and has virtually trained thousands worldwide
- Featured on the cover of *Direct Sales Diva Magazine*
- Her mission is to help struggling mompreneurs break through barriers and become the superhero God created them to be

Quote:

**"If you get the culture right,
success is yours for the taking!"**

– Jennifer Stroman

Coach's Notes:

Before we start, I want to say how excited I am for this specific chapter. With everything shifting online, more and more, many leaders have forgotten the value of events. Jennifer attends my masterminds and other events to level up her game. And she creates many incredible team events. At the time of writing this book, I am scheduled to speak for her team retreat next month. I can't stress enough the importance of doing events! And no, I am not saying to overdo them, but yes, you need to do them to build the proper culture.

How to build an unshakeable culture through events

Did you know that events are one of the best ways to help a struggling organization? In addition, 96 percent of small business owners say that company events produce a positive return on investment. Why?

Events instinctively create connections and provide a path to establishing great culture. It is where you form camaraderie. It's where you come together and find common interests, values, and world views. It is a way to foster an environment of collaboration.

Terrified! I was terrified, nervous, excited, and anxious all at the same time. These are the emotions I felt before attending my very first event. I wasn't sure people would like me. I stressed about what I looked like and what I was wearing. I am naturally nervous around crowds, so I worried others could tell I was sweating and panicking.

I went because I really wanted to connect with my leaders and sideline sisters. I wanted to learn more about the products, celebrate successes, grab the latest products launched and the exclusive swag given out during the event. I mean, who doesn't love a good deal and exclusivity, right?

As I settled into the crowd, I began meeting new people, learning who I bonded with, and finally got a feel for the culture of my organization. I felt comfortable, wanted, valued, and appreciated. More so, I connected with people on a deeper level. Not like we could while we were in the day-to-day grind - this was different. We bonded and exchanged contact information.

I learned so much about our company, my team members, and the products. My cup was filled with self-development, training, tutorials, and knowledge – it was an information overload but in a good way. They even had a fabulous launch event, awards ceremony, and party. There we celebrated, cheered each other on, collaborated, danced, and laughed until the wee hours of the morning. The energy was contagious, and I was hooked! I "drank the Kool-Aid," as some say in this industry.

Whether it was the cherry Kool-Aid or the fact that I felt like I had finally found my home in a company, either way, I was glad I got out of my own way, faced my fears, and attended an event. It forever changed me. It changed how I viewed this industry, my company, and my team.

Fast forward twenty-one years, and I am not with that company anymore. However, it set a foundation for me in this industry. As the years went by, events came and went. I learned what worked and didn't work for creating a monsoon of success on the heels of an event.

Teams with thriving cultures are more likely to be successful in their businesses. Recent research from Grant Thornton and Oxford Economics found that organizations with an "extremely healthy" culture were one and a half times more likely to experience more than 15 percent average revenue growth.

Organizations of any size can benefit from the connection, acknowledgment, recognition, and community that events generate.

It is crucial to invest in your team's culture, but *how* do you build an unshakeable culture through events? How can you advance your team's success through events?

I will break down three critical components to any event you attend or host with your team. But first, have you ever attended a company convention?

They usually have some type of classes or sessions for learning. Maybe a keynote speaker to get the crowd going. They also have some kind of entertainment. Perhaps a meal, cocktail party, DJ, band, or performance. And the group you attend with usually all wear the same shirt, color, or coordinate in some way that sets you apart while creating team camaraderie.

I have been to events where the teams are huge, and they take photos together, sit together, and some even have their chants or hand gestures. It is crazy but at the same time so much fun. As humans, we long to be accepted. To be a part of something more and events provide an opportunity to do just that.

Did you notice that I didn't describe an event as a sit-down learning or training session only? Events must be mixed with three ingredients to make them a success. It's these three pieces to the puzzle that have elevated my business from a full-time income to providing freedom for my family.

Before I give away my secrets, let me preface. This is to be used while attending a corporate event and for a team retreat or incentive trip. An event is an event, whether you plan it, your leaders plan it, or your company does all the planning. If you see a piece missing, fill that gap with the tips I provide below.

1. Training or learning sessions

It is essential to plan for training or learning sessions. This can be someone you hire or bring in to educate on a relative topic. It can be leaders in your organization that you want to spotlight and allow to showcase their talents. Or it can be a round table discussion where everyone is part of the discussion or topic. Maybe even a mix of all three of these options would work for you.

Hiring someone

When looking for someone to hire, find someone your organization would enjoy listening to or learning from. Do you know a coach in your industry? Is there a popular speaker that would motivate or encourage your team? Who is available to speak to your team? Be sure to schedule a time to talk to this person and describe what you want and expect from them. Be clear on what your objective is and give them a good view of your organization.

For example, my organization is primarily women of faith who are wives, moms and love to empower other women. Therefore, I am clear with my speaker or trainer that foul language is not appreciated. I wouldn't even hire someone I had to say that to, but instead, I would find someone who feels the same about empowering women and could respectfully motivate my team.

Leaders

Another great option is to ask someone within your organization if they are willing to share a particular topic. Most people will be flattered and honored to speak. So, if your budget doesn't allow you to hire someone, don't fret! You have some gemstones inside your organization that would love to step up and be a featured speaker.

Roundtable discussion

Last, you can provide a roundtable discussion. I love these discussions because you can ask a question and get multiple answers, responses, and reactions. It is enlightening to hear different perspectives and even engage in deep discussion about topics you may gloss over with a speaker. Even when I hire someone or have leaders teach my team, I always provide an opportunity for some hearty roundtable discussion time.

2. Team building activity

One of my favorite authors and mentors, John C. Maxwell, says it best, "Teamwork makes the dream work." To have a successful event, it must include a team-building activity. This will create connection and trust within your organization. Investing in a team activity and providing time for the team to bond encourages collaboration, communication, and camaraderie. In return, this leads to a stronger team, more motivation, higher morale, and better overall team culture.

The primary goal of team building is to create lasting results. Use a team bonding time to build skills like communication, problem-solving, and conflict resolution or simply to bring the team together. Maybe it is time to let loose and connect with fellow team members. Or maybe your organization needs to work on a collaboration, and an escape room where you come together to solve a puzzle is required. Either way, you know what your team lacks and what is required, so trust your instincts.

Selecting an activity

Every organization is different. Some team members may enjoy extreme sports and others a nice dinner show. It's essential to know the type of activities your team would enjoy and some teammates' limitations.

For example, maybe you want to have a fun relay race. Sounds good in theory, but can everyone run? How are their knees? Can they be in the sun? No, you don't have to cater to everyone's needs, but trying to be inclusive is always a plus! So choose an activity where everyone gets to participate actively. Even better if you can choose an activity that highlights their strengths while promoting collaboration.

Also, don't be afraid to ask other leaders who have successfully planned events what they suggest. Ask your organization what they enjoy or don't enjoy. Include them in the decision-making. You can even let them vote on activities. If you can provide laughter, excitement, a feeling of accomplishment and give them something to remember and talk about for years to come, you are on the right path!

What to avoid

The most influential events are memorable ones that leave a lasting impression. They lead to higher productivity, so be sure they don't feel like work. This is a time to bond, not learn.

One example of what to avoid is a leadership retreat I attended that included a lineup of training, breakout sessions, and more lessons to learn. Unfortunately, there was no break, a time to connect, or even downtime to absorb or process everything. This will drain your organization and leave them feeling overwhelmed and as if their cup never got filled.

Another example of what not to do is turning a team-building activity into a therapy session. Another event I attended turned into an emotional overload. The activities included digging deep into one's' psyche, and a lot of crying was going on. This is not a time to breakthrough limitations or walk on coals. Leave that to Tony Robbins!

An example that comes to mind of a memorable and lasting event I attended is a leadership trip we took to Vegas. We showed up on the strip in matching shirts and feather boas like we were part of a bachelorette party! The founders of our company joined us as we rode the High Roller and then went on a coach party bus that toured the Vegas strip, stopping at all the major sights for photo ops. We danced, laughed, jumped on and off the bus for hours, snapping photos at all the spots. This wasn't a learning lesson or leadership training, but instead, it was a time for us to come together, bond, and simply have a great time together. As I look back on this event, it was the highlight of our trip and a memory we still talk about to this day.

Get the best results

To create the best results from team building takes work when you get home. Everyone wants the high energy to stay alive but expects the energy to drop significantly when everyone initially goes home. The amount of training, celebrating, and "peopling" going on at events can be draining. So don't be discouraged if, at first, it seems like changes aren't happening.

So how do you keep the positive energy going?

Find ways to keep that excitement going. Challenge your organization to talk about the event, share the excitement with others. Create opportunities for people to continue to connect and interact in meaningful ways without the in-person events.

For instance, our team has weekly zoom meetings to stay connected. What I think has been powerful for our organization is hosting quarterly zoom events. These events include trivia, hiring a magician or comedian, or having a movie night together. It is a way to continue the connection long after an in-person event.

3. Celebrate good times – Come on! (cue the music)

Lastly, it's time to come together and celebrate your hard work as a team! Let off a little steam! Shake your groove thing and let loose. Celebrate, recognize and reward your organization for showing up, being committed, and achieving its goals.

Doesn't it feel good to be recognized for your efforts?

Everyone wants to be acknowledged and recognized. Some teammates might want a loud public celebration, while others may cringe at that thought, but everyone wants to be appreciated. It is your job as a leader to help them feel valued. A great way to do this is by taking time to honor their efforts. You can do this through a special awards ceremony, dinner with entertainment, or your team-building activity.

Awards ceremony

Ok, so this doesn't have to be elaborate like a company awards night. This can be silly, fun, and interactive. Your awards can be for sales, recruiting, or activity, but why not switch it up and make it memorable?

At our company convention a few years back, I had a mini awards ceremony the last night before everyone parted ways to pack and get ready to go home. We gathered in the hotel lobby, and I handed out awards for the goofiest things. For example, there were awards for "Barefoot Beauty" for the person who always took their shoes off, "Soccer Mom" for the person most likely to have snacks, drinks, and a first aid kit with them, and the "Dory Award" for the person most likely to be distracted. They were silly and fun. Everyone got a kick out of them. Of course, I also gave them certificates with their stats, sales, and recruits, but the fun awards were the ones everyone remembered.

Dinner with entertainment

Hosting a VIP dinner for those who have accomplished certain milestones is a great way to celebrate. You can even meet everyone attending the event at a local restaurant to hang out and grab a drink or appetizer. The best celebrations are those with some type of entertainment. You don't have to go all out. You can go to a show, attend a mystery dinner or even find a happening spot to eat that offers activities such as music to dance or games.

One example could be going somewhere fun like Dave & Busters to play games and eat. Another example I enjoyed was on a trip to Nashville. We found a fantastic restaurant with live music so that we could eat, dance, and listen to some great artists. Making memories *and* celebrating is always ideal!

Tied into team building

You can also tie this to team building. For example, our night on the Vegas strip celebrated our hard work and a way to let loose while building a bond and camaraderie. What better way to celebrate than to enjoy time together, laughing and bonding? That night we shared moments along our journey, remembered the ups and downs, and cheered all the success we achieved that year.

Take time to make sure your team feels valued because it goes a long way, but don't over complicate your celebration.

Bonus celebration tip: use words of affirmation

Isn't it wonderful to hear someone speaking highly of you? Whether during conversation or at a roundtable discussion, words of affirmation can be a highly effective way to make someone feel special.

I like to brag about individuals in a group while chatting. Or, as I am training, I point out a person's strengths paired with a compliment. Another effective way to uplift someone is by directly telling them how much you appreciate them.

Allow your leaders an opportunity to brag on their team. Open the floor to them to share with their team how grateful they are to have them there. Challenge them to be specific about each attendee on their team.

Each of these ideas is imperative to healthy, thriving team culture. By implementing these into your future events, you will see increased retention, activity, and motivation.

The best events I have ever attended or hosted have incorporated training, team building, and celebrations. These well-balanced events lead to an elevation in your success and take your business to the next level. It's time to build an unshakeable culture, and now you are fully equipped. I can't wait to watch your teams soar!

Coach's Notes:

What a checklist! I have never read this anywhere. All leaders know the value of events, and Jennifer just gave you the vision on why. She then broke down, even rarely speaking about minor details. If you aren't yet a leader in your mind, start with striving to have a small event. Let's call it a get-together of some sort, even if it is only three to four people. Everyone starts somewhere, and the only way you can get better is to start taking action. You will learn as you go, but the willingness to just do it is critical for you to have success. There is no way of creating a top-notch culture in my mind without some sort of event. Next, write a date down on when you will have your event or get-together.

JOANNA BACON

Achievements:

- Top online business coach for mums
- Mental health author
- Built 3 Multimillion Dollar Organizations
- Top of her company helping thousands become the good in the world

Quote:
"You must be the change you wish to see in the world."

- Joanna Bacon

When becoming a mum at sixteen years old, I grew up fast as I had to think about providing for my son. I had to get a job quickly and also attend college, and then onto university. It felt like a blink of an eye, and five years had passed. I remember thinking that I had essentially missed five years of my son's life just trying to provide a future life for him. I jumped straight into the nine to five full-time job routine and felt that same awful feeling as a single mum.

I was missing out on him growing up so that I could provide for him. I had such bigger dreams for myself and my son. I wanted to own a home, travel the world, and give Cam (my son), everything he wanted. None of that was possible if I continued to barely make ends meet at my full-time job. As much as I wanted that for us, I also thought that going to university and getting a full-time job were my only options. I didn't realise that there was something else out there where I could work flexibly around him.

I was working away from him so that I could pay someone else to watch him. After paying for childcare, there wasn't that much left, so it became a situation of scraping by to afford necessities and doing it all over again the next month. I needed more.

I wanted the freedom to experience being Cam's mum all the time and make money. I just had to figure out what that would mean. I can honestly say that I would have never had a second child if not for network marketing. I just couldn't justify what I had put Cam and myself through again with another child. I felt so much guilt and regret each day I had to be away from him for so long. Network marketing allowed me to be the mum I had always wanted to be, to my second son, Charlie.

I know that there are parents out there that probably have felt the same way. Maybe you are all in on the idea that network marketing can help you replace your income and create time freedom, but you don't know *how*. In this chapter, I will share with you one way I have found to help increase sales, create community buzz, and set up interest around joining your team. All of this is possible through monetizing a Facebook group.

What does monetising a Facebook group mean? Monetizing a Facebook group means that all of our sales pretty much come from a Facebook group. You are utilizing a free tool (Facebook) to advertise and market to a group of people that are a warm market. Warm means that they know you or are interested in what you have to say. There are several different ways and strategies to use Facebook groups. I will be sharing how my team has utilised Facebook groups to do successful business.

First and foremost, you have to create a group. Successful groups are active. The more people you have in a group, the more active the group is. I like to tell my team that their job is to load the group full of people. Whether you have one person on your team or five hundred, once you set up a group, let your team know that this group will benefit them and their business. In turn, it will help your team grow, so it is a win/win for everyone.

The Facebook group is there to educate people, share testimonials, share offers, create buzz, answer questions, and celebrate. We want people to use this group to learn about a product, use it, excel with it, and then make product sales. The most important thing about monetizing a group is knowing how it works. Not everyone is going to be added to the group and start buying products right away. Remember this!

Sometimes people start groups and get people in there, but they stop being consistent because they say it's not working. It won't work if you don't! People will start coming back in and reading more information. My team starts seeing more conversions and sales as they engage and interact with people and the Facebook group. People feel more comfortable in a group being an observer and reading information than having you spam their inbox and telling them you have something they need.

Algorithm basics

I'm not sure if there really are algorithm experts out there, but in the social media business world, we all need to learn the basics of how algorithms work. Algorithms connect people based on friends lists. If you have a viral post that is liked, shared, or commented on a lot, the algorithm pulls your post for more people to see. Some may not even be on your friend's list. The algorithm is all about getting more people to stay on the platform for as long as they can. For example, if I make a post in my Facebook group, my friends will start to see it pop up on their feed. And if someone in my team shares a post, and I comment, it will also be shared into my friends' feed. What's important here is that we are using third party validation to share with our friends, too.

Now, let's think about if I post something and everyone on the team starts engaging with it. I now have my friends and all their friends seeing the post. You can easily start getting more eyes in your Facebook group when you begin teaching your team about algorithms and how to use them so you all can benefit from them. The more team engagement, the higher chance that the post has to go viral and be put in front of other people. We are indirectly pulling people into the group by having great engagement in the Facebook group.

I have taught my team that if they are commenting on posts, adding to the group, replying to people in comments, and tagging people on posts, it will help get information to more people. It's such a great way to follow up indirectly and get information about the products.

Coach's Notes:

*I have one of the two largest **generic Facebook** groups in all of network marketing (The Game of Networking). I can count on one hand people that I would pay close attention to when it comes to FB groups, and Joanna is one of those. I have had the opportunity to coach her and watch her have continued success personally. True wealth is ability, not what you have in the bank. Joanna has successfully built three different companies, so it isn't about the right place or time. But she knows how to have success. Oh and on the fun side if you see a bunch of words that you think should have a z instead of an s that's because in the U.K. the claim they spell it properly and we don't in North America. Ha! Joanna is from the U.K. so we kept the for her in this chapter.*

Be the news

I have a lot of questions about what I think people should be posting in their groups. I like to think that I am a news channel. Every night when I was a kid, there was a news broadcast about the latest happenings and current events. They would also cover interest pieces, breaking news, the weather, etc. That is how you should operate your Facebook group for network marketing. You can share informational videos about the product, quick updates, science interest pieces about the product, customer testimonials, breaking news about the company events, etc. Basically, keep people coming back every single day wondering what the latest and greatest is for your team, the company, and the product.

One of my favorite ways to utilise the group is getting testimonials from your customers. Testimonials help use other people's experiences and their own words to help you sell your product. If a friend sees another friend sharing a testimonial on the product, it makes them more likely to buy. These testimonials can be updates on their journey or even just giving value to the group, so it could be that people are sharing recipe ideas for healthy meals. It could be that they're sharing their experience on using products or even just a demo of how to use the product. Just so that the customers can visually see what they're getting, how it tastes, how it looks, how it's used - all those things.

First steps to set up

You can do a couple of things to ensure that they are more likely to buy and engage with the group when people come into the group. First, create a welcome message that tells people what to expect from the group, or an introduction to your best sellers. Also, give people an outline of where to find important information in the group - i.e., product files and price lists in the guides section of the group. This way nobody is getting lost when they come into the group and wondering what they should be looking at first.

Another thing to do is set up admins. You should have a couple of trusted team members that are admins on the page. Set up ground rules for what you are looking for and what you will allow in the group. We don't allow spamming as a group, and we don't allow sharing things that aren't our products. Admins are there to help keep that culture going. I personally only let my direct leaders be admins so that we all know what to expect and keep the standards high in the group. Side note: I also have several people from different countries as admins. That means that when I am sleeping, I have an admin in the United States who can monitor things for the group. Train your admin team to know what type of posts and pictures are acceptable in the group and navigate when they must intervene and delete content.

One huge key to running a group is knowing where the sale is going. If I can give you one piece of advice, set a strict policy around sales within the group. As a joint group (meaning I have all my team leaders and their people), there could be confusion about who makes a sale. Part of the success of the Facebook group is your team knowing that it is a trusting community. No one wants to add their friends and family and then have someone else "take the sale" from them. Everyone in our group knows that customers will always be directed back to the person who added them to the group. If we can't figure out who that is, the person is handed to the admin, and we figure it out. This has created an enormous bond of trust in our group. They feel very confident adding people to this group and knowing that no one will be poached.

Creating community

Monetizing a Facebook group only works when you have created a great community around it. I know that my Facebook group isn't just about selling products. I am also building the culture of the team. Everyone needs to think about culture when building a Facebook group. You want to make sure that everyone's on the same page with the culture of the group. This includes how often you are sharing and what is included in your posts.

You need to know how to engage positively. It's not just me. It's a team collective because the entire team uses it, and the community has to be on board with it. Not everyone is going to use the Facebook group, and that's ok. But make sure that you create rules and policies that everyone can stick to and agree upon.

The biggest challenge to any group is making sure that people are constantly commenting, constantly sharing updates. It doesn't benefit anyone if I am the only one sharing in the group. If someone in my group wants to add all their friends and family to our team Facebook group, we can talk about what I expect from them as a leader. If they can contribute, they are welcome to add as many people as they want.

I do several training sessions around plugging into the Facebook group and being active in the group. If they want their friends and family to see the content (remember your basics of algorithms), they need to show up in the group and participate. I call this a content support group. We engage in content to support the group. If someone says they've added something in the group, I can jump on and add comments to boost the post. The algorithm starts building up.

Part of creating the community is also learning what gets it buzzing. Have you ever been around a beehive when it starts buzzing really loud? That's what we want to do with our Facebook groups! You can create buzz by knowing your community. What gets them excited and lit up? We love doing competitions. We are a competitive group, so I know if I create competition, there will be more buzz in the group. People tend to respond strongly to competition. We also do giveaways, and that creates a frenzy! Know how to use the buzz to your advantage. Part of the excitement of the buzz is not trying to do it all the time. Stagger the buzz so that the energy can rise and people don't get burnt out from it.

> **Coach's Notes:**
>
> *It is called **social** media. Too many people miss this whole section when creating their Facebook group. **Community!** This is how you create an online culture. This takes time, but it is how you can create a long-lasting online Facebook group. I have seen many Facebook groups start well, but only those with a community last. Creating a community needs to be a part of both the short-term and long-term focus.*

Benefit for the newbie

One of the biggest objections to starting a network marketing business is not knowing what to say and feeling like you don't have the experience or knowledge. This is one of the most significant benefits of a Facebook group. Whenever this objection comes up with my newest team member, I always tell them, "Not to worry. You have an entire community of experts supporting you and ready to answer questions for your new people." This has helped people start sharing from the beginning, knowing that they are adding their friends, family, and associates to a Facebook group that will be helpful and never cross boundaries.

The Facebook group also gives the newest people chances to join giveaways, competitions, and free products. It isn't always something that a newer person has the means to do. Being in a Facebook group helps them have the experience and resources they didn't have before. For example, someone who has just joined could add some friends, and then the next day, they could win a competition or get some free products. That is pretty amazing and helps create wins quickly for the new member.

Most people who go into the group for the free giveaway end up buying a product down the line, so it just ensures your whole target market is in the same place and has a great chance of seeing what you're offering.

My team has a straightforward way of adding people to our group. They send a message that says, "Hey Stacey! I don't know if you've seen but I am building up my business group and I would love your support. We're doing a giveaway for some free product this month. Can I add you in and count on your support?" It is that simple. They can also do a simple post asking who would like to win something for free - and get added in from there.

With the Facebook group, you can indirectly put that information in front of people, you know, if someone's talking about how they're not sure if something will work for them. Sharing testimonials of different people's success is powerful. People start connecting with stories and other people in the group that they wouldn't have access to previously.

I had somebody on my team sharing about sleep and how they've got great rest with their product. It captured someone else in my audience's attention, and she reached out to me and bought that product to improve her own sleep.

The group is vital for new people because it also gives them access to people who know the products inside and out. These people are sharing videos, and posts, and our most recent members are learning at lightning speed. People pick up on energy, and when you have created a community and sharing, people can feel that energy in the shared content. Don't use stock photos and fake posts. Use real people, do video, be authentic.

I love getting a new member on a live stream with me on their public Facebook wall. This helps get exposure with their audience, and we can drive people to the group from there. The idea is to drive their network to the group to see the testimonials and interactions happening in the Facebook group. I'll interview them and ask them how they feel about the product. And obviously, that helps them get out there. It helps their social media interaction, and it helps their friends see what they are doing live. Another crazy outcome is that every time I do a Facebook live with someone, we both get pop-up orders and an influx of friends who come into the group. So once again, another win for the team!

When people first start in the industry, it can be overwhelming. They're waiting for those sales, and often they give up before those sales come. The Facebook group helps them create community quickly, have the experience instantly, and have a great place to put people and follow up without spamming them.

My friend Stacey had never been in this industry before. She follows the system and plugs and plays people into the Facebook group. She is now earning about $1,000 every month by literally plugging people into that group and being active within that group. That is the power of monetizing a group.

Another friend Lysia had never made much money in Network Marketing and has now used this simple step by step tool and sold over $50,000 worth of product in the last year!

Exponential growth

I have always been a hard worker. I have always been willing to go out there and hustle and share what I am doing. But I know there is no way to build the business I have without monetizing my Facebook group.

In the first year of monetizing the Facebook group, I have made well over $100k in personal sales. Just last month, I sold over $10k worth of products. I wouldn't be able to do that if I wasn't using this group. The amount of information you can get out in a group is crazy. You can constantly be sharing, and Facebook utilises the algorithm to pull it into people's newsfeed. You don't have to hammer them with it or be spammy yourself. It gets people to pop up in their newsfeed. Facebook groups helped me build a great customer base, and I've never had a customer base this big. I've never had a repeat customer base this big as well! This all comes from monetizing the Facebook group.

To see the exponential growth, you need to be willing to follow up. People don't follow up after they have shared information with people. They don't get the sale because they didn't follow up and check to see where their customers are. You will never be successful in this business if you don't follow up. You don't always have to follow up and ask people to buy but checking in with people can lead them to your page and content, and they sound find their way back to your group and products!

Most people don't realise that it might take five interactions before you get a sale. It's been really good for people to plug people into this group so that they can see who is interacting, what posts they are interacting with, and have a great place to comment and follow up with them. The group is also a great tool to follow up. If you know someone is interested in a particular product and then someone else posts a testimonial about it, you can tag that person, "Hey Rob; we were just talking about this." "Hey, Dean, check out this post!". You can keep follow up within the group.

My first three months in network marketing were hard. I spoke to over 300 people and sold some shockingly low numbers. I remember thinking that I had been sold on a dream that was now my nightmare. I was mortified at being rejected over and over again. But the glimmer of being a full-time mum kept me holding firm. I like to say I was *ignorance on fire.* Once I started to do what you're supposed to do, implement the steps, and do the self-development, I began to get more from it. Utilise the steps. Start to use Facebook groups to make money and be consistent at it. You really can be the person you want to be and make money.

Coach's Notes:

Throw out all of the strategies from this book and focus on one part of what Joanna said. "I spoke to over 300 people and sold some shockingly low numbers." This is a top leader giving you the behind-the-scenes uncut reality. No strategy will ever overcome your lack of reaching out to new people!

JORDAN LEVECK

Achievements:

- Wife and momma with a slight Harry Potter obsession
- Lost 155 lbs. & became a trainer & nutritionist
- Top earner with a multi-million-dollar team
- Top recruiter with over 1,000 people personally enrolled
- Personally sold $50k in customer sales in a single month
- 725k+ followers on TikTok

Quote:

"Stop putting a ceiling where God put a sky."

\- Jordan LeVeck

What is consuming you?

Before you were born, God set you apart. The problem isn't that you are unworthy or incapable. The problem is that you keep forgetting you're the opposite. Or maybe you've never completely understood your inherent greatness. Either way, I'm hoping to help you remember what you were put here to do and give you some actionable tools to help you stop hitting your head against the wall and generate some massive freaking results. Ultimately, I'm hoping to help you shock yourself with what you are capable of – the same way I did.

If you told me at nineteen – when I was 300 pounds, suicidal, and my idea of a good time involved sleeping with random men, eating until I couldn't feel, or getting drunk and chain-smoking – that I'd be where I am now, I would have slapped you. I would have straight-up laughed in your face.

That's the problem with humans. They are consumed by fear and limitation unless they train themselves to transcend it. And that's some next-level Jackie Chan nonsense most people aren't willing to commit to. I will share how I grew a 7-figure business not despite my fear, but because of it. How I went from broken, depressed, and wanting to quit network marketing because everything I built fell apart to creating massive duplication and success in this industry is a story I love to share.

Also, since this intro is so heavy, I feel compelled to tell you that A.) You have a nice butt, and B.) I'm a hot mess express – so don't compare yourself to me for one second, unless it's to realize that if this weirdo can crush it in this industry, you freaking can too.

Coach's Notes:

Jordan is the absolute queen of referral marketing. This makes a few of my awesome friends mad, but I believe she is the very best at referral posts. I also believe that this is the next big thing. Referral posts have only caught on with a few companies. But, done right, this is the game-changer idea that could make all of the difference.

How to 100x your business with referral marketing

Now, outside of working when you don't feel like it, it would be referral marketing if I had to pick one thing that made the most significant impact on my business growth. I always say, "Keep the main thing the main thing." What I mean by that is spending 80 percent of your time online focused on the activities that make you the most money and 20 percent with your team. Most people have this backward. They build a team and then get into management mode. They think their job is now to motivate their team and tell them what to do, to keep them working. That is what you need to be doing with *yourself*. If you want *beach* money, you need to always be in launch mode. Rob calls this point in your business where you start getting bossy and stop getting results the "sophomore slump".

If you have never had success in network marketing, that means you never *started* focusing on the most important things for your business. Stop lying to yourself if you have had success but feel like you are in a "funk." You just quit doing what brought you success in the beginning. So, what are those things? IPAS!

IPAS = Income Producing Activities

These are the things that lead directly to *money*.

IPAS are essentially the activities that create the highest return on investment of your time.

This is the opposite of busywork. This is the stuff you do if you like money. Do you like money? I do! I even sell a shirt that says it. Is it kosher to write "lol" in a book? I'm going to say no, and we'll pretend that didn't happen. Moving swiftly forward.

When things slow down in your business, it's always because of one of three things.

1. Mindset
2. Method
3. Season

Mindset becomes a problem when you find yourself getting stuck in your head – you need to get out in the world and act, even when you don't want to. Method is a different beast entirely. It is the *way* you are working your business when you *do* work. I am here to tell you that "You can't say the wrong thing to the right person" is 100 percent BS. Sorry. It just is. I would consider myself the "right person" in this industry, and you can definitely say the wrong thing to me.

Now, that's not supposed to terrify you. Of course, you are *going* to mess up. But there are more people than mistakes you can make, so it's all good. The idea is to learn by doing – to "fail forward". We learn how to walk by falling repeatedly. Toddlers are like tiny drunk humans smashing their way through life, learning how to be a person. That will be you in this industry, friend. Learn how to laugh and celebrate the action you take instead of the results you get, or you are 100 percent doomed.

Rather than obsessing over "Is this the perfect message to send?", "Is this the perfect post to put up?", "Would this person even be interested? They are so successful!", screw all of that and rip the Band-Aid off. Try things in batches and then taste test it, like you're making muffins.

Betty Crocker never *hated* herself for needing to tweak an ingredient. Stop doing that. If the method isn't quite working, make informed tweaks. It's not a reflection of your competency or self-worth as a human being if something needs updating. *You have to be willing to suck at something long enough to get good at it.*

The cool thing is, the more action you take, the more you celebrate said action and don't destroy yourself for *learning*, the quicker you improve. If you send three perfectly crafted "A+" messages, you *might* get a response. If you send out 100 "B-" messages, no one will die, but you'll also have a way higher chance of getting results and helping people.

Point being? You have to stop demanding or expecting perfection because no one else demands that of you. We need to normalize that you make up in numbers what you lack in skill! You have to get *messy* to grow. I'm sharing what works with you, but you'll have to mess around to find how it works best for *you*. I am going to teach you the principles that will help you shorten the learning curve, though. The method I use and teach my team to use is the following:

Daily method of operation for future millionaires

IPAS/The Main Thing – 80 percent of the time

1. Referral posts

2. Ask the extra question

3. Follow up

20 percent of the time

4. Curiosity/Attraction marketing

5. Create conversations

6. Love on/empower team

My team hears it repeatedly. Referral post, extra question. Referral post, extra question. *Until you die.* Just kidding, kind of. Until you get rich, scratch that, **forever.** I am having too much fun writing this. But listen, these two *simple* activities could transform the entire trajectory of your business. So, what are they? The best income-producing activities known to man, in my humble opinion.

Remember how I told you I sold $50k personally in a month? Referral posts are how I did that. TikTok is how I sell now, but that's a conversation for another day. Referral posts are the *best* strategy to create leads (and eventually sales), start conversations, make new friends, and market your business without relying on only *your* network. This means it's an effective strategy for *anyone*, new or old, with or without influence, and it creates massive duplication. TikTok doesn't do that yet. I'll get there and create a system around it, and you will all get the course from me once I do, right?!

Let's talk about what a referral post and referral marketing are. A referral post that someone else puts up for you on their Facebook (or IG/TikTok) is about your product or service. Pretty freaking simple. But the power of this is *huge*. It's like having that person open their Rolodex of contacts and handing it to you. It's putting a *ton* of eyeballs on your product/service that wouldn't have seen it otherwise. Even if that person has 500 friends, and only 5 percent of their friend list sees it, that's still 25 people you would not have been able to advertise to without crawling in their inboxes like a spammy butthole asking for a favor. Referral posts are *money*!

Not only do they get you leads, but they also get you *targeted* leads. People are raising their hands, saying they are interested in what you have. It is so much more powerful than adding random humans on Facebook in the hopes of selling them crap!

Here are some statistics to support the idea that referral marketing is the way of the future.

- Twenty-eight percent of millennials say they will not try a product if their friends don't approve of it
- Word of mouth is the primary factor behind 20 to 50 percent of purchasing decisions
- Businesses with referrals have a 70 percent higher conversion rate, and 69 percent faster close time on sales

- When referred by a friend, people are 4x more likely to make a purchase
- Customers acquired through referrals have a 37 percent higher retention rate

Sign me up, am I right?! But there is a right and wrong way to go about this. So, let's talk about strategy. There are lots of ways to get people to put up referral posts for you, and not one of them involves begging or asking everyone and their mom to post because it benefits *you*. Instead, you must make it something that benefits *them*. The only exception to this is "Ride or Die" posts, which I'll outline below.

Coach's Notes:

Let's put this in perspective. A vast majority of Jordan's business was built on referral posts. She is not only generating new leads, but she is creating **targeted** *leads. These are warm market leads. So many network marketers sponsor like crazy, but then it stops there. This brilliant referral post strategy can create insane duplication. Don't stress it if your first attempts aren't great; just like everything, you need to commit and keep improving it until it is dialed in. Follow Jordan's formula. Now let's learn* **how to**!

How to get referral posts

1. Ask your ride or dies

Message friends or family, aka your "hot market," something like –
"Hey NAME! I wanted to ask a huge favor because you've always been so supportive of me! I started a new business a while back that got me super excited! I was just wondering if you'd be willing to throw up a

simple post on your Facebook for me to help me out! I'm *not* asking you to buy anything, haha. But it would really help! Would you be willing to do that?! No worries if not!"

2.   Referral post giveaways

Every single month on my team, we do a team-wide giveaway for referral posts. You can do the giveaway yourself *or* with your upline for their whole team and have several leaders chip in.

Examples Giveaway Items: bottle of your most popular product, $200 amazon gift card, $50 Target gift card, Apple Watch, etc.

What to do: Do a giveaway post and/or live video on your timeline

People who comment, message them -

"Saw your comment on my giveaway post! Have a second to get entered now?"

Then reply to their comment and say, "Messaged you!"

When they say "yes," here's what you say: "Perfect! To be entered, I will send you a simple premade post, and you just put it up and tag me in it! That work?"

3.   Ask your current customers

Current Customers example script: "Hey NAME! How the heck have you been? I am super excited; I'm doing a giveaway this month for __! You are eligible to be entered. Do you want to be included?"

If they say "yes," use the same script as described above on the giveaway script.

4.   Ask potential customers or marketers

You can use the same script for potentials that you use for current customers!

Do's & don'ts for successful referral posts

Let's talk about *what* to have people post. Once someone agrees to throw up a post for you, you're going to send them a picture and text to post with that picture. The best referral posts are typically posts about your flagship products, aka your most popular products.

- ✓ Do: Make it look like the person posting is posting it themselves. Like a normal human! Use humor. They're curious or intrigued about it. It should *not* be easy to tell they are posting to promote or sell.

- ✓ Creates/piques curiosity because they don't have all the info. If you saw it, you'd want to comment, "What is that?"

  You don't post the company or product name. Instead, use curiosity & attraction marketing! I won't cover that now, assuming you already know what that is, but it's highly effective!

- ✓ If it's a customer posting, they can share a personal before and after and their positive experience so far!

Ask them, "What do you love most about what you're using? What positive things are you experiencing so far?" Then use their words to create a personal post! For example, "Well, I was really skeptical about this 'waist trainer in a bottle,' but *insert a snippet of their testimonial* and end with something about how they are now a fan/officially obsessed/etc.

Example: "Well, I was really skeptical about this 'waist trainer in a bottle'... But I've noticed my appetite has gone down, and I love food. Lol. Also, my pants fit better already, so that's a win! So, I am officially a fan."

They could post this with a spoonful of the product they're using, and voila! Creates curiosity, shares benefits without pitching, makes people want to ask for more information!

- ✘ Don't: Have them post a before and after photo of someone else

- ✘ Use a pic with words/graphics on it

- ✘ Use a CTA (call to action) like "comment ___," "reach out to ___," "get with my friend ___," etc.

- ✘ List a ton of benefits and ingredients (looks salesy)

- ✘ Approve all posts onto your timeline

- ✘ Expect every post to blow up/think you're failing if you don't get immediate sales. The purpose of referral posts is to get people into your "funnel" or your Facebook group with info about the products/ business. Then, you have an extensive list of people to follow up with when there are new products/sales/promos/giveaways, etc.!

   Also, that person's Facebook may not get good engagement, and you can't control that!

- ✘ Continue doing posts that haven't worked over and over. Tweak anything that doesn't work.

- ✘ Do the exact same wording/pics every time. Use different pics and change the wording a bit from person to person.

The people who comment, you'll reply to their comment and tell them you'll send some more info, then message them and use the exposure process your company suggests! For example, in my business, we use the ATM method. This means we have Facebook groups with more information about the products and business, and we "Add," "Tag," "Message." Add to group, Tag in info, Message with someone who knows more than you to help close.

Become a recruiting machine

Once you have people throwing up posts for you, how can we take this to the next level and use this same strategy to bring on new team members? It's really simple. All you do now is throw in the extra question and teach your team to do the same. Just ask the referral poster if they're open to taking a look at what you do! The format looks like this.

1. Meet them where they're at

2. Compliment them

3. Throw in the extra question

4. Give them an out

Example script: "Thank you so much for posting. I appreciate it! Listen, I know you may not be interested, but I just love *insert a genuine compliment about them*! Would you be open to checking out how I'm making money doing this? No worries if not!"

If they say "yes," you will follow your company's exposure process to point them to a tool like a short opportunity video, ask them what they liked best, then introduce them to an upline or people who know more than you to help you close them! You always want to point to a tool, never *be* the tool. Don't word vomit and try to explain everything to them. As soon as you open your mouth, you are training someone. If you give them all the info, they are going to think, "I don't have the time to memorize all of that info!" If you point them to a video explaining it for you, that can be duplicated.

You can also throw in the extra question when people engage on your posts or watch your stories! Just say, "Thank you so much for watching my stories/for the love on my post!", then add the extra question, a compliment, and an out!

At the end of the day, the person who asks the most *wins*. So really, your goal is to be an *ask-hole*. See what I did there?

Now, if this was helpful for you, and you want *more* tips, I'm not going to go on and on here – there are too many legends with big things to share! But, you *can* always follow me on Facebook and TikTok! I have an entrepreneur training group called Mother *Hustlers*, linked on my Facebook bio with more free training on this that's open to everyone, so feel free to stalk and check it out!

The caveat

The secret to true success is simple, and I have had to learn it repeatedly, both in this industry and in life. You have to show up and do the most important things, whether or not it sucks that day - *especially* when it sucks that day. Action is the antidote to fear.

And listen, I get it because if overthinking or ruminating made you money, I'd be next level rich. But you can't solve a problem in the same place it was created. A problem in your mind must be solved in the *world*. You can't *think* your way out of feeling "stuck." You have to *act* your way out.

So, what does this mean for you? It means that sometimes, you just have to smack yourself in the face and make yourself do the most important things, whether or not you feel like it. You have to tell the mean girl or dude in your mind, "Not today, Satan, we have sh*t to *do!*" No one who has accomplished anything worthwhile did it because they have a gene you're missing. They simply decided to show up when it felt crappy. They were certain they deserved the outcome, not because they felt like taking action. Know that you deserve to win.

You have to do it because you deserve it, not because you feel like it. Period.

And even when you get where you're going, success won't "fix" you. Even after losing the weight and building this incredible business, I had a lot of emotional trauma to sort through and unpack. (Therapy is a freaking Godsend). I didn't get there and suddenly felt healed. You won't, either. There is no rank or dollar amount that will heal you or make you feel worthy. You are worthy *now*.

Contrary to popular belief, however, you do not need to *heal* to grow. You do not need to *heal* to succeed. You just need to start where you are, hands shaking, voice trembling, and take massive imperfect action.

You just need to stand up, take a step, repeat. Over and over. And I'm right there with you, friend.

Coach's Notes:

Jordan said it best, "Action is the antidote to fear." You won't be perfect ever. You won't be great at first. No one becomes great without sucking at first. As you read Jordan and these other legends' chapters, know that they were bad before they were good. The difference is they took massive deliberation. They failed their way forward. Whichever strategy you choose will take both urgency and patience. Everything worthwhile is always harder than we think it is going to be. I can tell you this: **it is worth it.** *I highly recommend that you implement the referral marketing strategy.*

KELLI JOCHUM

Achievements:

- Top leader in network marketing and top 1 percent in her company

- Homeschool mom of three leading by example in the balance of all things work and home

- Positive energy, encouragement, and the ability to help others grow in confidence have helped her continue to grow a dynamic sales organization

- Proof that you genuinely can design the life you want if you're willing to put in the work

- If your success isn't fun, you're doing it wrong

Quote:

"If you don't sacrifice for what you want, what you want will become the sacrifice."

Coach's Notes:

*Before you start reading Kelli's excellent chapter, know this. Months ago, I didn't know Kelli and had no idea if Kelli felt fear or was just good and manipulated fear to drive her. At the last Leader of Leaders Mastermind, there were 40 top leaders from all different companies. Kelli knew no one! She decided to come one week before it started, and by the time the mastermind was over, she had made more new friends than anyone else in the entire Mastermind. She wasn't loud by any means. She just seemed fearless, but that wasn't the case. You will learn later in this chapter about her thoughts on the word **fearless**. All leaders have different fears, but the best leaders hit those fears head-on! Let's learn how Kelli attacks those fears head-on.*

Kelli's Story

We all experience fear. Does it make you want to run away sometimes? Or maybe all the time? That is certainly our natural instinct, and for a good reason! However, in this chapter, you will gain insight on different types of fear, how you can use it to your advantage, and maybe even call it friend. But first, a story.

Sleepovers were one of my favorite things growing up. Whether they were at my house or my friend's house, it didn't matter. What mattered was spending tons of time with my buddy, having all the snacks and laughs possible. I've reached my thirties, and that part hasn't changed. I still totally do sleepovers. But now it's family sleepovers! Yep! My husband is game, so we load up the three kiddos, and of course, we never forget the dog. Yes, we bring Daisy to hang out with her doggy friend #DaisyandLuluforlife. We all spend the weekend living that saying, "eat, drink, and be merry." Well, all except Daisy.

At a recent sleepover, I noticed that Daisy would be right under my feet every time I got a cup of water. She would just stare at me. It was a desperate, begging type of stare. I checked the doggie water bowl, which was plenty full. I showed her where it was and then carried on about the weekend shenanigans (it was a bottomless margarita and Jurassic Park marathon kind of day.) The following morning, I woke up and took Puppers out to take care of her "business" (Puppers = Daisy, our dog has like six names, doesn't yours?)

Instead of sniffing about and finding the perfect spot to bless the earth, she went straight to the side of the kids' play equipment to lick every drop of dew and rain off it. But the water bowl was full! It was the gravity water bowl where you fill the jug and tip it upside down. These dogs weigh like forty-two pounds when soaking wet. There's no way they could have drunk it all. I went back inside to check, and sure enough, it was still full! I brought her over to it and sat with her for a moment to see what was going on.

She slowly drew near to it, head down, then backed off. The other dog, Lulu, with her cute, little sassy self, came over and drank right out of the bowl, which caused it to make that "glug, glug" sound. Crazy Daisy totally freaked out, and then I realized that's why she was so thirsty! She was afraid of the "glug, glug." Wow. My Pupdog would rather die of thirst for an entire weekend than get near that "water monster." She'd rather sacrifice a life necessity than face her fear. If you know me, you know nearly everything goes through my brain filter and comes out as a life lesson. I mean, I'm a homeschool mom. Always seeking those teachable moments! In that moment, I couldn't help but consider how many times I let fear get in the way of what's important to me. Have you been there before? Have you ever gone out of your way or maybe even gone through pain so that you didn't have to face your fear?

I went straight to Google to do some research to figure out why we as humans, and animals for that matter, are so fear adverse. My first step was to define fear. I had heard some fear acronyms (false evidence appearing real; "f" everything and run) but never had taken the time to look up the actual definition. According to the almighty Webster, fear is an unpleasant, often strong emotion caused by anticipation or danger awareness. Certainly, the water jug wasn't going to cause danger for Daisy Dog. When I'm trying to help my kiddos understand a concept, we break the sentence or idea down to a simple SVi (Subject, Verb-intransitive.) Fear is an emotion. Lightbulb (said in my best Gru voice.) This was life-changing for me.

I had always made fear out to be the "bad guy." I would train, "Your fear is stealing your joy! Fear will take your next win if you don't stop it! Don't let fear rob you of your best tomorrow!" Yep, fear was the guy wearing a dark mask abrasively barging in unannounced, ready to take everything away from me. As this belief played out in my life, I eventually learned to overcome my natural response, which was to "run." My learned response was to confront fear in a state of defense and "fight" the fear.

I reached some huge business goals I had for myself with that state of mind. But, my friend, let me share from experience that if we continue just to fight our fears, we will end up so exhausted. I mean, think about it; fighting is exhausting! Whether it's physical or mental, a fight might fill us with adrenaline while it's happening; but we can expect a crash afterward. And the longer the fight, the longer the recovery period will need to be. Theoretically, this is why so many entrepreneurs hit a certain point in their careers where they burn out. But each new step on that income ladder, each new title earned, each new experience brings this emotion of fear, so they fight it and keep going.

How am I supposed to lead this team? How is it possible for me to give each person the care and attention they deserve? What if they don't like me? What if they do like me, and then I let them down? Am I even qualified to have this title? How can I manage this responsibility and still be the best mom, best wife? Do I even deserve this income? Am I using this income wisely? Is that investment really worth it? Is this even what I'm supposed to be doing?

Have you had any of those thoughts? It's so easy to quickly label them as "negative thoughts," as if "what if they don't like me" is a bad thing to wonder about. Let's consider this. What if the reason we become overwhelmed with thoughts of not being good enough is not a "bad" thing? What if it's because we are just good people? Would a "bad" person care what someone thought about them? Probably not. Would a "bad" person care about continuing to be a good mom and wife or wonder if their investments were a good use of resources? All of these questions that so many of us ask in fear are actually a reflection of being a good human!

Ok, so what if they didn't like me? What then? I could fill in the blank with a plethora of worries. But, what if all of these really are *not* fear of the unknown but fear of the *stories* that we put in place of the unknown—all of the "what-ifs."

We let our thoughts take the pilot position, and we fly all over the place, coming up with stories and creating visions of horrible outcomes. I'm not going to tell you, "Just visualize the good outcomes and make yourself believe good things will happen," because that doesn't work long term. Instead, I'd tell myself, "Don't fear, Kelli! You've got this! This is all just fear trying to steal your success!" I didn't realize that I was digging myself into a dark pit with those words. What were the wins worth if I were constantly battling myself?

Fear isn't something to fight. Fear isn't a bad guy. In fact, quite the opposite - fear is your friend.

Before I continue, I must apologize for every time I told someone, "Don't be afraid." That's like telling someone to dismiss their emotions. Fear is an emotion, remember? So, I may as well say, "Don't feel the way you feel," or, "The way you are feeling is wrong," or, "You should not feel shame." Telling a child who believes a monster is under their bed, "Don't be afraid," doesn't make them less scared. It just covers their fear in shame. Now they feel scared *and* ashamed of feeling scared.

I also must apologize for every time I told someone to "be fearless." Some people will just dismiss fear and say, "fear isn't even real," or "pretend like you don't feel fear." I'm sorry, but when I was about to stand up in front of 100 people to speak, I felt fear, and it was real! I'm pretty sure the gut-wrenching urge to vomit wasn't from the previous night's dinner, ok? Burying emotions (burying fear) leads to repression. It's like junk mail - at some point, you're going to have to deal with that pile; otherwise, it's going to stack up and take up tons of space.

As a part of our perfect human design, fearlessness is quite literally *not* an option. We have this remarkable part of our brain called the amygdala. The purpose of these clusters of nuclei is to tell us when there is danger. If I walk out my front door and there's an alligator on my porch (yes, this happens in Florida, very rare, but it happens), my amygdala is going to send messages to the rest of my body to GTFO! We have fear for a reason! It is a gift to us to keep us safe. Fear is our friend.

Here's the kicker – our amygdala doesn't have the power to distinguish a life-threatening fear from a life opportunity fear. A life-threatening fear looks something like starvation, fire, zombie apocalypse, lions and tigers and bears, oh my! A life opportunity fear looks something like starting a new job, speaking in front of the class, writing your first book, driving for the first time, going on that first date, or moving to a new city.

When I'm getting ready to go to that interview for that new job, my brain is going to receive the same signal as if I were chillin' on a mountainside suddenly confronted by a hungry bear. No matter what, we will feel fear. It is a part of who we are. "Fearlessness" is not an option. Fear is a natural emotion. It's there to keep us safe. So come on, everyone, say, "thank you, Fear, for keeping me safe!"

But what about when the fear we feel is the life opportunity kind of fear? As I write this just for you, you fabulous human, I'm feeling some fear! It's entirely natural for me to have thoughts like, "What if no one appreciates what I have to say? What if they think I'm a dummy? What if no one actually does have six names for their dog?" Okay, that last one isn't actually a fear, but some things are definitely triggering my amygdala! But how do I keep writing to deliver this to you? How do people scale their business to seven, eight figures, and how can people travel solo across the country? How do climbers reach the top of the mountain, and how do people do big scary things even with fear trying to keep them safe?

These five words will change the game for you as soon as you believe them. "I'm afraid, and that's OK." You can acknowledge the fear (feel it, name it), and you can even "Do it scared," but fear must be accepted to get to the next level without baggage. Fighting fear will leave you burnt out. Denying fear will lead you to shame. Being fearless is a fallacy. Accepting fear as a part of who you are will break the chains and take you to a place where you can use fear to your advantage.

When you must speak at your friend's wedding, or you're ready to accept a big promotion, or you make it to the final round of a competition, if you feel fear, it is not a sign to run for the hills. You have an advantage now. Now you know that it is a sign of life opportunity. When I feel that fear, now I know it's just an emotion sending me a message that things might change a little bit. Things could be different as a result of what is happening. Because that would be unfamiliar, I may start to feel unsafe.

Because there is not a life-threatening danger, now I know this fear is just warning me that I'm heading in the direction of growth.

I love a nice breakdown that I can take with me and easily remember. Maybe you do, too! So here are the three steps to becoming friends with fear and using it to your advantage.

1. Acknowledgement

    Thank you, Fear, for trying to keep me safe.

2. Acceptance

    I'm afraid, and that's okay.

3. Action

    Take the next right step, one at a time.

I can be afraid and still be freakin' Wonder Woman. I am just stronger now because fear is my sidekick. When fear walks in the room, I have a seat ready for it. So have a seat, fear. Let's do this.

Coach's Notes:

Fear! It is an illusion. It is the story we tell ourselves that decreases it or enhances it. Think about it. If you are making new invites to a prospect and you start to wonder about all the worst-case scenarios, your fears increase to the point they feel real. The worst-case scenario feels so real that your emotions make you **feel** as if it already happened. Whereas when you shift that story to the worst-case scenario, it isn't a big deal if someone says no, and even better than that is focusing on all the reasons they should say yes. You control the stories you tell yourself. Those stories mold many of the decisions you make daily. My favorite part of all the fear teaching from Kelli is how she makes fear not that big of a deal. She mentions accepting the fear many times and just moving on with some sort of strong power statement in your head.

LORI HAYES

Achievements:

- In Network Marketing for 20 years
- Built 2 different network marketing business to the top level of the compensation plan
- Has built an organization to over 30,000 strong in more than 30 countries
- Earned 30 sales incentives in 20 years
- Chosen by corporate executives to serve on the first Advisory Council for her previous network marketing company
- Top 3 Leader Award in company in a combination of Leadership Development, Team growth and Sponsoring
- Speaker at numerous company conventions and leadership events
- Owner of Mindset and Success Coaching Business

Quote:

"Whether you think you can or you think you can't, you're right."

- Henry Ford

Be brave, not perfect – how simple actions can take your business to the next level

What if a simple challenge could help people get past some of their basic fears and blocks? They could easily start to do simple things that would help them move forward in their lives and business. This challenge would be easy to implement and would build community, strengthen bonds among your team, and the effects would last for a long time. You would say, "Give me some of that, please!" Get ready because that is exactly what I created with *Be Brave, Not Perfect*! Let's dive right in, and I hope you enjoy this as much as I have.

I did a fantastic team challenge all centered around *Being Brave and Not Perfect* in a Facebook group. We asked people to do simple things in their business and life every day, even if it seemed scary. We gave them a deadline that meant that they could not procrastinate and had to just do it. Finally, we asked them to share their experiences in our group so that others could gain strength from their actions. The result was nothing short of amazing!

People who had experienced a disconnect from their business and the team all of a sudden came around! We saw lots of enrollments and promotions for months and months after! To this day, well over a year later, when someone does something scary, they will share their *Be Brave, Not Perfect* moment in our group, encouraging and helping others to take that next step! It is truly empowering!

Coach's Notes:

*This is a fascinating insight. I remember doing a zoom coaching call with Lori and her sharing with me the success she had with this particular challenge. I think that we get so fixated on just the business skills that we forget about some of the basic principles that make all of the difference. For example, being brave and not perfect on the surface sounds like common sense, but when we inspect our lack of action, we realize that what we think we know and what we do can many times be completely different. The phrase "**be brave, not perfect**" helps us to focus on taking action. It helps us to focus less on the result and more on the process. Successful leaders are **process**-driven. Lori is one of the very best experts on mindset in the entire network marketing profession. Observe the next several paragraphs closely to see what you need to level up your mindset.*

More from Lori

Being brave is doing scary things outside of the comfort zone—Having courage when facing uncomfortable situations despite the fears. My take on why the change: Being brave doesn't mean there isn't fear. It's doing it anyway. We each decide what bravery is based on our past experiences and habits. For one person, being brave might be talking to the person behind them at the checkout line, and for another person, it might be speaking to a crowd of 1000 people. At the end of the day, growth is experienced when we decide to be brave in our business.

Fear is inevitable. It is something that everyone will feel and go through. When we understand that, we can move through it so much faster. Often, we listen to the head talk telling us loud and clear that it's not safe to move forward. We listen to the talk in our heads about how we will be judged, fail, or even be rejected. The fear is so powerful that it makes us move right back into the place we've always been. We know we don't want to be in this place of fear, but we usually don't know the action required to get out of it.

All of this makes sense because rarely does anyone ever talk about what that voice actually is. That voice is merely a program in our mind taught to us from past experiences. When we understand, we must choose between running the old program or writing a new one. We are no longer slaves to our thoughts. We can choose to feel growth and freedom! We have choices!

There is fear that keeps us safe and fears that keep us stuck and frozen. When a snake is in our path, or we're coming to the edge of a big drop, we will experience the fear that helps us stay safe. However, the fear you feel when you decide to invest money into a class for personal growth or when you decide to speak at the event or even talk to the customer you love about becoming a builder is normal and controllable in your mind. It will happen every single time you start to up-level or do something out of the ordinary.

In your everyday life, you have a routine and a way of doing things. Your mind and BODY become familiar with being comfortable and content. Let's call that X-type energy. Now, you have an idea that pops into your mind to do something out of your comfort zone. You start to look at this idea and run it through your mind, but it seems like it may be hard, or you are not sure how you could do it. As soon as you *decide* in your mind to do the hard thing and become emotionally involved with it. It changes to a different energy. Let's call it Y-type energy.

The X and Y energy try to come together, but they clash, creating a colossal disturbance or chaos in the body. In the chaos, fear, and anxiety show up, and all the head talk that goes right along with it. You'll think things like: "What was I thinking?" or "I can't possibly do that!" or "Who do I think I am?" You know the head-talk, the panic that sets in and makes you rethink your decision to do something new and significant. It will happen *every* time you are comfortable (X energy), and you decide to become uncomfortable (Y energy). It's in knowing that you can take personal power.

The awareness of what is going on in your mind will change it all because then you can understand that what you are feeling is normal and all you must do is keep moving to get to the other side. There is *no* danger. The only danger is deciding to succumb to the thoughts, fall back to your comfort zone, and stay exactly where you are now forever. Once you understand this is normal, you'll start celebrating fear because it means growth is happening!

It is *so* exciting to make that decision to follow your intuition's nudge and move through the fear. You'll be amazed at how you will feel! It's like a wave of joy because you did something hard and scary! And here's what is so cool, the next time, it won't be nearly as hard or scary because you've already done it! Here's the thing, eventually, that new idea (Y energy) that you moved into becomes the norm, and then you're ready to up-level again!

That is being brave, and it can make huge shifts in your life and business.

Let's talk about perfection. What does perfect even mean? "Perfect" is free from defects, so says the dictionary—excellence in every part of a thing.

Perfectionism is something that many people relate to. I know I do. I was so good at putting on a show. No one knew my faults because I covered them *so* well. Any time someone came to my home, it looked like I lived in perfect order. In my business, I studied and prepared and studied some more so I would look like I knew it all. I spent a lot of time working on things to make them look perfect. I acted confident, but inside I was a mess. I thought I was doing a good job by being a perfectionist, but it held me back.

Perfectionists try so hard because they lack a positive self-image, have high standards, and stress more than others. Even when something was done beautifully, they will focus on all the things that weren't perfect. They don't enjoy the process of growth at all. If they do fail, it can be disastrous, often tail-spinning themselves into a depression where they can take days or weeks to recover. They procrastinate because they don't want to do it unless it is perfect. This isn't productive in the long run. Part of the fear is being "found out."

I lived the first forty-eight years of my life in this cycle of perfectionism. I was working with a network marketing trainer when I was a top leader in a previous company, and I remember so clearly her saying to me: "I've never worked with another top leader who lacked self-esteem to the degree that you do."

Those words were so painful to hear! I knew it, but no one had ever said it to me. It was my worst fear coming true. I had been "found out." It took me many more years to break free from that pattern, but I can tell you, freedom is attainable. Today, I am forever grateful for her being bold and speaking those words to me because they changed everything. I knew something had to shift, and she was honest and truthful about what that something was.

When you are brave and not perfect, you can get things done quickly and easily. Imagine getting everything you need to do done quickly and easily! *Yes!* Productivity is at an all-time high! I have found myself getting a full day of work done in only four hours when I implement being brave and not perfect into my routine.

Here is the secret: Do all your high-impact activities during your best hours of the day and do not procrastinate. Remember that word? I like to call my best hours "Power Hours." They are from 8 am to 12 pm. I can rock almost anything out during that time, and when I remove all distractions, fear, and perfectionist tendencies, I get it done, and I get it done quickly! Your hours might be from 8-midnight, it doesn't matter. Just *decide*, remove distraction, say "no" to the voices in your head holding you back, and *do it*!

When I started doing this, my business completely changed. I went from making low six figures a year to mid-six figures a year in just over a year and a half. I reminded myself to be brave all the time. As a matter of fact, my word of the year was courageous during that time frame because I had to keep it right in front of me. Trust me; the fear has never stopped popping up! And it never will because I will *always* be up-leveling, and so will you!

Here are some of the *Be Brave, Not Perfect* activities I like to do during those Power Hours of the day.

I have found that spending at least 30 minutes doing a specific task with no interruptions is a good benchmark but dedicating an hour at a time is even better.

Any type of following up or prospecting is vital to your business. For example, I love asking for referrals. I made a list of over 130 people to call and ask for a referral, specifically for building referrals. I'll be letting them know why I'm reaching out to them, and then I follow up if they say yes. Do this in your power hours!

Here is what it looks like, "Hi Suzie, I love how connected you are and how successful you've been in real estate, and I know you run across so many kinds of people. I'm looking for a highly motivated person who wants to become an entrepreneur and change their life. I'm willing to invest time and resources into the right person, and I know you know people like this. Would you be open to sharing my information with anyone who comes to mind?"

I also take this time to book events and network with other people. Any way to stay in front of people, I will be doing it. I will do some social media during this time; however, you mustn't start scrolling and go down a rabbit hole. Stay focused and do what you need to do, and then get off.

In these cases, having a timer is super effective. I don't like to use the timer on my phone because my attention goes to something else once I pick up my phone. So, I have a timer I purchased on Amazon specifically for productivity. It has 10, 15, 30, 45, and 1-hour timers on it. Set it, and don't stop until it goes off! It is *so* freeing knowing you don't have to worry about spending too much time on something. Your brain can relax, and you can focus for that time.

Productivity tip: Make a list of your top income-producing tasks in your own business and focus on those in blocks of time. Be brave and not perfect, and get it *done*! Your business will explode!

As you coach your team, remember that even the team members who seem insanely confident may lack a positive self-image when they have perfectionistic tendencies. So how do you start to change your self-image? One way that I love is to imagine yourself how you want to be. I went through this process myself; I was a huge perfectionist/procrastinator. However, once I identified what I was doing, I wanted to change, and I wanted to change as quickly as possible.

As a certified mindset coach, one of the key things I coach is to focus on, visualize and attach emotion to what we want to create. I wrote down who I was as God created me and who I knew I *had* to be to achieve my goals. Then, I visualized myself as that person every day. This visualization was detailed, including how I looked, posture, spoke, and interacted with people. It is imperative to add how it felt to have the level of success I was dreaming of and how I made decisions.

Before long, I found myself doing these things in my current life. I found myself showing up in the same ways I had imagined. I stood taller, the brave came in, and the procrastination and perfection went out the door. So what if it wasn't perfect? So what if I was open and honest and vulnerable? Guess what? People connected with me more and more, and everything changed. I started seeing the level of success I had been imagining.

If you are unsure how to start this process, look at the qualities you like in successful people you know. It's important to not go into comparison mode but simply pay attention to what you like about those role models. Maybe it's the way they look you right in the eye when they are talking to you, the confidence they show when talking to a group, or how they remember people's names and speak their names often.

When I was going through this process the first time, I had a few role models I used. I liked the way a particular person was engaging and making the people they were talking to the most important people in the world at that time. They focused and made people feel important, including me. I remember walking away loving them even more than I already did! I pictured myself doing the same things. In my visualization, I would feel the joy the person in front of me felt as they talked to me. I had served them well! I stood taller, spoke clearer, and shared my passion.

When I made decisions, I just trusted my instincts all the time. Those are all the things I witnessed other people I admired doing, so I decided to do them too. As I visualized myself doing these things and feeling excited about it, all of a sudden, opportunities came up, and I rose to the occasion without even thinking much about it. I had changed the program in my mind because I practiced it so many times that my body knew exactly what to do when the time came. That is the beauty of the subconscious brain. All those times I was visualizing and attaching emotion to the visualization, my subconscious mind thought that event was happening! Like I already had that experience! As I moved through my real life, those characteristics became *my* characteristics!

They actually teach this to kids and young adults who play sports. There is not a superstar athlete who hasn't imagined themselves catching the ball or making the shot at the last second to win the game. When they get in those circumstances during an actual game, their body knows what to do! This is such a powerful technique that at the Winter Olympics in Sochi, the Canadians brought eight sports psychologists with them. The United States brought nine, including five that were specifically for their ski and snowboard programs. They would record themselves going through the track, starting with standing on the hill. They would feel the wind on the back of their neck, and they could hear the crowd cheering. Then, they would imagine engaging their core and seeing exactly how they wanted the jump to turn out. Over and over, they would do this, preparing for their time to win the Olympic medal! It is the power of visualization with emotion that elevates them to be the best in the world.

We can use the same techniques in our own personal and business life, and we should! Imagine what it looks like to show up confident, brave, and consistent in your business. Imagine the powerful person you are, the powerful influencer you are. Imagine hitting that next rank or being recognized by your company or, even better, cheering on your new builder as they are recognized for their accomplishments!

We started this talk by discussing the simple challenge of asking the people around you to do simple things to overcome basic fears and blocks. So I walked through being brave and letting go of that perfectionism and shared my journey with you. Be Brave, Not Perfect was a download God placed in my heart, and I took immediate action with my team. It is a blessing that has changed many lives already and will continue to change lives for a long time to come. I love to see someone sharing a challenge they are facing, and someone says, "Hey, be brave, not perfect, you got this!" This is the beauty of a community loving and growing together.

You can only create what you *believe* you can create. And it can all start by simply being brave and not perfect. That one action can change the trajectory of your business and your life. So what will your next *Be Brave, Not Perfect* moment be?

Coach's Notes:

*I had so many reminders and even new takeaways from Lori's section, but the sentence that jumped off the page for me was this "**Productivity tip**: Make a list of your top income-producing tasks in your own business and focus on those in blocks of time. Be brave and not perfect, and get it done! Your business will explode!"*

*Let's dissect that part. Most of us know that we waste so much time. We make the plan for the plan of the plan of the plan. We say we worked so hard, but we only invited two or three new people at the end of the month. We were fake working! We were confusing being busy with being productive. We were spending too much time studying the compensation plan and anything we possibly could to simply avoid doing what we **knew** we should have been doing. If you follow this one productivity tip and nothing else, your business will change forever. So let me repeat it in my own words. First, you should list out any income-producing activity you can. What is going to make you **money**? Then go to that list and prioritize it. Now assess how much time to spend on which activity. I recommend spending 80 percent of your time talking to brand prospects of customers. Now schedule it. **Now just go do it!** This plan will take your business to levels you never imagined possible. The question is, are you going to do it?*

LYNN COOPER, RN

Achievements:

- Top 1 percent in her company
- Six-figure earner
- Ten years of network marketing
- Former ER RN for twenty-eight years
- Loves to volunteer third world medicine, especially during a crisis

Quote:

**"People don't care how much you know until
they know how much you care."**

- Theodore Roosevelt

The path isn't always a yellow brick road

If you told me 15 years ago that I would be a full-time Network Marketer, I would have told you that you were crazy and that I am not that "kind of person."

I was programmed to believe that you go to college for X number of years, graduate with massive debt, then work a job for the next forty years to pay off the debt and retire, finally. So that is what I set out to do. But, unfortunately, it felt like that was the yellow brick road that I and everyone else is supposed to follow.

I always loved to help people. Early in my childhood, I felt compassion for anyone who was ill or hurt. I knew by age sixteen that I wanted to be a registered nurse. I also came from an abusive home, and I wanted to leave it as soon as I turned eighteen. So, I left home, went to nursing school full time while also working full time. It wasn't easy, but I thought that if I was going to continue supporting myself, I needed to push through it. I finished my RN degree and worked several years in an intensive care unit, and then twenty-eight years in an emergency room. I was on the exact track that I had always thought that I was supposed to follow.

Ten years ago, a friend asked me if I would like to try a product sample that would help me lose weight. I said sure, as my doctor just told me my cholesterol was higher than normal. After all, what woman doesn't want to lose weight? I liked its taste and thought, why not give it a try versus taking a prescription. I had great results, and people noticed and asked me, "How was I doing it?" The product was from a network marketing company. My mantra had always been about helping people, so I went from a product user to a distributor! I saw the opportunity to share with others and also get paid! I began my network marketing journey in 2011 part-time while working as an ER RN full time.

Being determined to become a top leader, I watched and studied successful people in that company. As a result, I was awarded *Distributor of the Year in 2013*! The odd thing was that my paycheck didn't match that award. It felt to me like the "Good ole Boys Club" with those at the top making all the money! Meanwhile, my team and I were out there busting our butts! It didn't make sense, but it confirmed my suspicions.

I never shied away from hard work but always believed that you should be rewarded fairly for your efforts. That was not happening, so I pretty much gave up on Network Marketing! I was putting in way too much time and not earning what I would expect. My sponsor quit - leaving me in 'an inside, inside leg' with no upline sponsor other than an egotistical master distributor. Plus, I disliked all the hype that I heard from their top leaders about how you can make $10,000 a month when they were the only ones earning that! I was the person who would talk about helping people make $500 a month, a much more realistic target. Then my situation changed.

In 2016, while exiting a parking lot in Orlando, I was struck on the head by a closing parking gate. I was losing strength in my arms and legs. After being misdiagnosed with Multiple Sclerosis by three neurologists, I had a recommended cervical spine surgery. Unfortunately, the neurosurgeon accidentally paralyzed my right vocal cord and damaged the other. I was being sent to doctors all over the US for evaluations. There was talk about performing a tracheostomy to protect my airway, which is putting a hole in your throat to enable you to breathe.

I developed deep feelings of anxiousness and sadness as a result. I recognized the symptoms and knew if I told my doctor about it, he would follow the usual medical practice by prescribing "pills" for me and probably lots of them! Thus began my search for a natural remedy. I started with some vitamins that our local nutrition store recommended. It did nothing for me. In 2018, a friend of mine in California offered to send me some CBD from his dispensary. I was open to plant medicine but declined as I wanted to get it the legit way. I saw a local medical marijuana doctor in Florida and was approved for my medical marijuana card. I purchased the marijuana CBD that the doctor suggested. It helped me, but it was way too strong for me! I adjusted the dosage and could not find one that didn't turn me into a couch potato! I then began my research as I knew everyone couldn't be walking around stoned.

Two months later, I found a brand with hemp-derived CBD that checked off all my boxes, and that wouldn't get me high! I received my order and started using it right away. After two servings, I felt a sense of peace and calmness that I hadn't felt in a long time. A feeling of being "safe." As an RN, I thought perhaps it was a placebo effect as I wanted to feel better. After my third serving, my husband said to me, "Your eyes are sparkling." I asked him, "What do you mean?" He said, "You look happy again." I told him I felt happy again. It was at that point when I thought, "If this just helped me, then I need to go all-in and share this with as many people as I can." That sparkle in my eye turned into a flame that got me passionately fired up again to get started back into network marketing!

The yellow brick road path to success had taken me far, but it wasn't all it was cracked up to be. It wasn't until I was given another option that combined my love for helping people *and* creating time and money freedom that I felt like I had truly found my path - the path that was genuinely for my family and me. That can be you too. Maybe you are one of the people on the yellow brick road of a 9-5 job. Perhaps you have found network marketing, hoping that it may be your true path. In this chapter, I will talk to you about the biggest shift in my network marketing journey and how it helped me go from the skeptic to the top one percent earner in my company.

Coach's Notes:

Lynn is like many of us in network marketing. She wasn't sure if it was going to work. She is now a top earner but at one point says she pretty much gave up. This is another reminder that everyone has greatness in them, and it is another reminder that success isn't easy and to keep pushing forward. Lynn also said this, "I watched and studied those in that company who were successful." This is a massive key to success. To have success, you have to **pay attention***, learn and then* **implement***. By repeating this process over and over again, you will improve. Eventually, those subtle improvements lead to* **success***.*

Change your mindset from recruiter to consultant

I wanted to talk about shifting your mindset from being a recruiter to being a consultant. I was inspired by a training from my mentor Jenna Zwagil, the #1 Female Top Earner in Network Marketing, to write about this subject. Thank you, Jenna!

Over the years, network marketing has gotten somewhat of a bad rap as some have a negative connotation around recruiting or being that salesperson. People see you as someone trying to convince you to buy something – like a used car salesman with a plaid suit or the many annoying telemarketing calls we receive. Shifting your mindset to the frequency of being a consultant will get more people attracted to you.

Think about it when you are looking for a solution to a problem – would you rather talk to a recruiter or a consultant? Most are leery of a recruiter. A consultant focuses on educating their prospects by giving them recommendations based on their expertise.

There are many consultants in all kinds of different fields out there. For example, your car is having a problem. You make an appointment at a garage and tell the mechanic the issues that you are experiencing. He writes down what you say and takes a thorough look at your car. Then he gives you a call with his recommendations to fix your, car along with his estimate to repair. You then give permission to get the repairs done.

As an ER RN for twenty-eight years, it was natural to interview patients to get their history and describe their symptoms. Collect their information and find out their problems. Being a consultant in network marketing is similar, but it is essential to have a different mentality and mindset. You must have some knowledge and expertise in your products, services, and the opportunity for success in your company. As a consultant, you will listen closely to your prospect, take notes, share your story and other stories, offer product recommendations, and answer any questions about the business. Then bring in an 'expert' or use one of the tools available for third-party validation.

Becoming a consultant is all about helping people and showing them that you have their best interest in mind. A recruiter is going to have their own best interest in mind. This is a simple shift that I made from going from recruiter to consultant in network marketing. It was incredible to see the shift when I would introduce people to the product and business opportunity when I figured this out.

Here are five steps to becoming a badass consultant in network marketing

- **Build rapport** with your prospect by building a relationship with them.

We are in the people business. People like to do business with people they like and trust. Don't spend too much time in the "friend zone" building rapport. Also, don't be fake about it. Be authentic. Break the ice and get on the same frequency that they are on. Take the time to find out what your prospect's problems are. Ask them questions. What are your goals? Your dreams? You want them to feel that they can trust you with this information. Write down all the "symptoms" they give you. Get to know them. What are their dreams? Do they have kids? Any pets? Do they need permission from their spouse? What are their health goals? Do you have a job? Find their needs. Find their motivating factors. Find their hot button, the thing that fires them up.

- **Give full disclosure**

Let them know that "I am not here to sell you something that you don't need or want. I am only here to match products, services, and opportunities to what you need."

- *Product selection/solution*

Be sure you have all the information that you need before you make your recommendations. For example, "You said that you wanted to make $500 a month because you want to get your car payment paid for, right? You mentioned that you have three children that you are homeschooling. How does your husband sleep? You mentioned that one of your health goals is to lose 20 lbs." Then let them know, "Based on the information that you have given me, I recommend…"

- **The close**

Many in Network Marketing freak out about closing. If you do the first three steps correctly, the close is super easy. "If I can show you a way to achieve weight loss and more financial independence for that $500 extra you said you needed…" "So, if I can show you a way to do these two things, would it be safe to assume that this opportunity makes a lot of sense for you now?" Go through their objections and show them how they can overcome them. "Money– don't worry about it as that is the exact reason why you need to take this opportunity right now. You need to do something different, right?" Let them talk about their objections as objections are often like a therapy session, helping them overcome their doubts. Be in control of the conversation while being a good listener at the same time.

- *Follow-up* is the most important part of the sale as soon as they get started.

Ask them to commit and put their awareness in for the next 90 days. Also, ask them to agree to commit to you as their leader for the next 90 days.

Give them a blueprint of what they are going to do. Help them select products or services. Let them know the best package to come in on to make the most money, so they don't leave any money on the table. Help them set up their auto-ship. It would help if you stayed on the phone or be with them during this process to help them navigate their new back office.

Set up an appointment for the next day at a specific time. Ask them to write a list of 25 people that they know. Tell them not to prejudge anyone as they write their list. It will amaze you who will order or become a top leader in your team that you may have initially discounted!

Inform them how to use you as a leader. You are not their boss and will not harass them to get out of bed to build their business. That's something that they're going to have to do for themselves. Let them know that you will cheer them on, clap for them and announce their rank recognitions as they hit the ranks. Ask them to use you when they have questions, need a three-way chat, or call. Let them know that this is important as they are brand new and don't have credibility yet.

Let them know you will add them to some social media groups, and you will talk with them tomorrow at our agreed-on time. We will talk about your personal development plan because this business is super dependent on it.

Coach's Notes:

*These five steps are pure fire. Shifting from a **recruiter** to a **consultant** is like shifting from leader of followers to leader of leaders. It takes time, just as every new skill does, but it creates so much leverage for your team and company.*

More from Lynn

Make the shift to a consultant

As a consultant, we are just literally bettering their lives while at the same time we are bettering our own life. So, the benefit is still there for us, but it isn't all about us.

Remember, your job as a consultant is simply to ask questions and identify a problem that your prospect has and if your products or business opportunities are an excellent solution to that problem. Then you ask them to make a purchase. If it's not a good fit, let them go! This will be a timesaver and protect your reputation. Taking your eyes off yourself and focusing on your prospect's needs will give you better results.

This past year and a half have shown many people that working from home is the better way! For many months, "work from home" was the #1 search on google trends. Shopping online has also become the new norm! This movement will continue to get stronger!

Your mindset is a set of beliefs that shape how you make sense of the world and yourself. Having a positive mindset in Network marketing is so very important. Think about how you see yourself in network marketing. For example, if you think your job is to be a recruiter, you will find yourself following a very different path than if you believe your job is to be a consultant.

As I shifted my mindset to be a consultant rather than a recruiter, I began to understand that what I did as an ER RN for the past twenty-eight years was super connected to being a network marketer. I would interview the patients, and along with the doctor, we would look for problems. Find their pain points, then find the solutions to help them. Network marketing is no different. Look for the issues which you are going to help solve. Realize there is no problem that does not have a solution. If you start with the belief that every problem has a solution, then the power of expectation will assist you in finding the ideal solution for your prospect.

I challenge you to take action - listen intently to your prospects, interview them to find their problems, their pain points. Then, be a consultant that provides the solutions for them.

The good news is that the better you get at solving problems, the more money you will make.

I wish you all the success that this beautiful life has to offer!

Coach's Notes:

Thanks, Lynn, for laying it out in such a structured way. One of my hidden insecurities, when I started network marketing, was becoming just a recruiter. I believed that a recruiter just recruits and then abandons their team. You will learn about systems in this book, and combined with that and becoming a consultant, you can build a massive organization. Don't allow your doubts of not being good enough yet to prevent you from taking action now. Stick with it, and you will get there.

MISS MARILYN

Achievements:

- Network marketing with her company since 2013

- Bought her starter kit as a dropout single mom with her last $300 while on the verge of suicide

- With her twelve-year-old autistic son, Maveric, at her side, she has created a powerhouse network marketing family of tens of thousands of hot pink feather boa-wearing members

- Went from destitute to the second consultant ever to receive $25k and $50k bonuses in the company

- Created a multi-seven-figure business while cheating death in 2019

- With her second chance at life, her mission is to leave a legacy of faith & love

- Several media outlets, including *ABC, NBC, Inside Edition*, and *Good Morning America*, have followed her journey of having a positive attitude in the face of struggle. She also featured for her coaching program "Star In Your Own Life!" where she helps people transform life from rags to rhinestones

Quote:

**"You must choose faith over everything &
star in your own life!"**

Coach's Notes:

*I seldom start writing something before an author's chapter has begun but **stop**. I want you to re-read a portion of Miss Marilyn's bio: "Bought her starter kit as a dropout single mom with her last $300 who was on the verge of suicide." Stop and think about this. Miss Marilyn was as low as one could be in their life. She was on the verge of suicide and now is one of the top earners in this profession. This isn't to say her journey was easy. This isn't to say your journey will be easy. This is to give you hope that anyone **can** make it in this business. I know that sounds cliché, but I firmly believe that. I have seen all different walks of life succeed. I have seen different ages, races, and genders have success from all over the world. First, you need to **learn**. Second, you need to take **action**. Part of learning is taking action. Spend 10 percent of the time learning and 90 percent of the time taking **action**.*

Walking in faith to build a network marketing business by Miss Marilyn

Most people don't believe me when I tell them this part of my story, but all of it is true. When I was in my early 20s, I caught on fire. It was a severe accident, and I feared for my life. I burned my face, hair & chest, and I was told I would not make it through the night in the ICU. As I lay there in the worst pain of my life, I realized that I was way too young to die. But there I was, burnt on most of my body, in an ER somewhere in Las Vegas, and I was utterly alone. There was only one thing I could do. I prayed.

The following day, I wasn't sure if I woke up or was dead and surrounded by angels. The most handsome doctors surrounded me, all in white coats, when I opened my eyes. I will never forget thinking, "If this is heaven, then I am good! I can definitely get used to this view!" As you know, I didn't die, but I was surrounded by doctors that were genuinely angels on earth. They spent exhaustive hours around the clock saving my life.

On that day, I made a very conscious choice. I chose to walk by faith. That day and that experience were horrific, and I realized that if I could choose to walk by faith even in that situation, I could choose to do it every day regardless of what I am going through.

Now, I want to clear something up before talking about how walking by faith can help your business. This experience was one of the worst of my life, but just because I went through that doesn't mean that I now graduated from the hard, complicated, and sometimes downright terrible things in life. I have contemplated if the world would be better without me and if my children would be better. I have faced more demons than there are feathers on a boa, and there have been countless times since that I have contemplated suicide. But through all of it, I have chosen to walk in faith.

Let's talk openly about network marketing. It is one of the best businesses on the planet! I genuinely believe this. But building a network marketing business isn't always about smiles and laughter. At times it is going to seem like a series of consistent bad days. You may cry; you may be questioning yourself. You may feel foolish for the way your friends and family look at you or, even worse, give you a pity smile when you talk to them about your opportunity. There may even be laughter, and it may be strangers laughing in your face! I promise you that you will want to quit on yourself at least once, if not a dozen times, while you are building your business. But you, my new beautiful friend, you must keep walking forward in faith.

What does it look like to have faith in business? Why would having faith as I lay dying in a hospital room help me build a network marketing business? Faith, by definition, is "complete trust or confidence in someone or something." So, when we are talking about faith, you must genuinely decide where you are going to put your trust and confidence. When I was in that ER wondering if I would make it through the night, I prayed to God and put all my trust in the higher plan He had for my life. I believed and put confidence in that whatever was going to happen was God's will for me.

Coach's Notes:

*Faith is one of the essential topics to understand when it comes to success in anything. I love how The Bible mentions, "Faith without works is dead." You have to believe in something you aren't positive of yet, but at the same time, that belief needs to be strong enough to get you into action. Miss Marilyn has inspired thousands of entrepreneurs through her **faith**. She has taught principles that are deeper than just network marketing, which creates both culture and leadership. Throughout this book, increase your **faith**, your belief and your action.*

More from Miss Marilyn

As you start to build your business, you will need to find something, someone, or a higher power to put your trust and confidence in. None of us can do it alone. You will encounter a plethora of struggles as you go through life. But, as you build a business, the choice of faith over everything can carry you through! Faith is magical!

I have had a life of so much loss. I have dealt with chronic illness, health issues, including a head injury and multiple hospital stays. And all of this has happened while building a multi-seven figure business. People always ask me, "How are you even doing this right now with everything you are personally struggling with?" The answer is small and mighty. "I have a mustard seed, and I am not afraid to use it!"

In Luke 17:6, the Lord said, "If you had faith like a grain of mustard seed, you could say to this mulberry tree, 'Be uprooted and planted in the sea,' and it would obey you."

A mustard seed is so small. Small enough that many people overlook it and don't think much of it. Many people are looking for the big, bold, brand new thing to get them motivated and on the right track when they start network marketing. Ahhhhh, but mustard seed faith is not for the weak. It may be small, but it is mighty. Using your own mustard seed starts by looking at your own trials and weaknesses. Where do you find yourself afraid and stuck? Write it down! To gain your own mustard seed, you must know what you are facing. You must first understand what you are facing.

Stuck is like the perfect living room with the most comfortable recliner, your favorite drink & snack, and you are binge-watching the hottest show. Stuck is the ultimate place where people fail in business and life. I like to say that, "Stuck doesn't suck." It's comfortable, familiar, and doesn't offer too many hardships. Stuck is the definition of mediocrity. Stuck & rock bottom are two very different places. Rock bottom is dark, empty, and desperate. People will do whatever it takes to get out of rock bottom. But Stuck doesn't suck. It cradles you into submission.

Get good at being honest with yourself. That mustard seed knows it's small! It owns it completely and knows what it is on this earth to accomplish. You, my friend, are on this earth to accomplish something. What is it? What are you here to do? If you don't know yet, that's ok. Use your faith to find out. You must learn to "Star In Your Own Life!" God has sent us here to star in our life. You should never be an extra! Ask God how you can stop being stuck and step into the role to become the star of your own life. If you have faith, even a small little bit, He will help guide you to your life's purpose and help you plant that purpose in the right spots.

Once you have identified where you are stuck, been honest with yourself, and asked for help, next, you must stare your trials in the face and walk right through them. Sounds simple. Sounds small. But just like the mustard seed, this is mighty. The biggest hazard people find in network marketing is getting stuck in comfortable places. It is easy to NOT talk to people about your new business. It is easy to watch Netflix instead of offering opportunities.

Walking through trials means that you have got to remember to wake up and intentionally walk in faith. You are made to be fabulous! Fabulous comes in all shapes and sizes. There are immeasurable possibilities you could inadvertently miss if you do not continue to walk in faith.

I always had a belief that I was God's practical joke. I thought I was made to play small, be a nobody, and live in despair & strife was living my best life. I didn't even understand limitless possibilities. I didn't think gigantic dreams were for someone like me. Can you relate? To this day, I still have to work on fully grasping the concept that dreams come true, and with God's help, I am unstoppable. However, I consider myself an expert in walking in faith. Daily I have to get up intentionally and tell myself, "Don't get in your own way. Don't block your blessings!" I forge my way through struggles, grief, depression, and I focus on my mustard seed of faith.

Right now, I am issuing you a dare! You can do it right now, as you read this book. I dare you to start making mustard-seed-based choices. That means to pick the thing that terrifies you. Yep! And then do that thing, like you know it's going to work out! Tell yourself that you are holding onto the confidence and trust of the mustard seed that whatever is supposed to happen will happen.

Recently, I bought a 101-year-old building, or a pile of bricks stacked in wall formations, that needs a massive renovation to become a state-of-the-art training facility & mecca for Acts Of kindness. Meaning, this small, enchanting town in Southern Alabama is laced with folks who spread kindness daily, and there will be special events focused on the spread of kindness. It is the kindest area in the USA! One of the sage older men in this Hallmark movie town at the beginning of the construction where the building is located in Southern Alabama says to me, "Single women don't usually renovate buildings alone."

I responded, "I am not alone!"

There was silence. He may have thought I was crazy, but I know who is standing with me.

I am walking in faith & our Heavenly Father is walking right with me. I have no idea how to renovate a 101-year-old building in need of every single renovation you could imagine; however, I do know I have the faith to make it happen. And I will.

It is hard going through unpleasant or horrific experiences. I know. I have been there more times than I can count. But I also know that you can choose to move forward in every single experience you are having. I know tremendous grief and sorrow as if it was my best friend. I know heartbreak and illness can cause you to get stuck & I also know you can pull on your big girl or big boy panties and create a phenomenal business and life filled with accomplished dreams.

It is not easy, especially at first. Walking in faith does not have to mean giant leaps. It can be baby steps. You see, as long as you are taking steps forward in faith, you are growing. Just keep moving forward. Resist the urge to sit comfortably or turn and go back.

I have a small glass jar with a single mustard seed in my office right behind me on my shelf. It is a constant reminder to use my faith. I have carried it with me in my pocket and taken it to meetings. I use it to remember to base my choices on faith.

I read this story recently, and I think it's just perfect here. "My father-in-law has a difficult time keeping up with writing pens. 'Seems like I lose them all the time,' he says. He will pick them up at hotel rooms, and he even will lose a hotel pen. Then, about 20 years ago, a good friend gave him an expensive pen set. He was excited about this wonderful new pen set. But he was afraid that he would lose them, just like he had lost all the other pens. So, he put the pens neatly away in a safe place. For the past 20 years, they've been safe but not used."

Sometimes our fear of a loss or failure keeps us from using what we have, our talents, resources, or achieving our hopes and dreams. Fear can sometimes paralyze us. However, the most significant loss is that for 20 years, the purpose of those pens was lost to safety.

Your most significant loss may not be a failure but your failure to use what you have to be who God created you to be. "As each has received a gift, use it to serve one another, as good stewards of God's varied grace." 1 Peter 4:10

So how does this all relate to building a network marketing business? Easy answer- no matter what, you just keep going. You cannot let anything stop you. Your faith must be mighty. So, keep telling your story, and keep pitching your opportunity. Keep believing, as your life depends on it, that you will build this business. And then do not give up.

When you get to the point where you think it's never going to work, that's just the beginning of where your faith is needed. We don't require faith for the things we know. Faith comes in for the times when we can't seem to see the ending. You can't let the naysayers get in your head. They are just steppingstones in your faith walk. But, they are the stones that will eventually build the foundation of your business. The trials will not stop & your faith will be tested, and you, my beautiful brother or sister, will keep walking. Think of it as a parade, wave, bless and release. Just keep parading. If you do not quit on the route, you will quite literally get the trophy.

I love getting trophies in network marketing! Those trophies come in the form of big checks and gigantic dreams fulfilled. They symbolize lives changed for the better. They symbolize faith! There is no reason you can't start earning your own trophies in network marketing.

I was in a horrific car accident a few years after I caught on fire. This accident, once again, dramatically changed my life. It could have been the end of my dreams. However, I knew what to do. I walked forward in faith.

I have struggled ever since. I have had folks tell me things that could stop me right there in the middle of my parade. But I dug deep, battled my 'mind monsters', and walked in faith. It took over 20 years for me to accomplish my goals, but I did it. Over twenty years is a long time to parade with no trophy. More than two decades – *let that sink in!*

Would you continue to strive for your goals for over twenty years? Or would you just sit in the family room of stuckness? Seriously. Could you keep parading? The parade will build your business; the family room will keep you very comfortable. But I can tell you, no one ever gets a trophy for binge-watching shows.

The trophies come from inspiring and serving others—those who choose to get on your parade float, so to speak. I want you to continue to wave at those on the sidelines, keep asking them to get on your float, but focus on those who got up & got on your parade float. Those are your people.

Those people are your tribe, link arms with them, and continue to walk in faith!

One of the primary keys of walking in faith is to **celebrate!** There are a lot of celebrations on this faith walk. Every time you turn a corner and see your mind monster zombies and charge forth, I want you to celebrate yourself and the choices you are now making based on faith! You can do this! Cheer for everyone, especially yourself! Learn the art form of being happy with your steps forward. Do not wait for anyone to celebrate you! This is your walk in faith. Celebrate you. You are a badass faith walker! I am so proud of you, and you deserve it all.

Get a fancy coffee, buy a new shirt, buy yourself flowers, new socks, that lip gloss or car part you have been wanting, and reward yourself for your faith!

When I am terrified and think there is no way even my mustard seed can handle the mountain in front of me, I dare myself to do it. Dares are badass and sexy, so that's why I dare. There ain't nothing sexier than a man or woman walking in faith and making it happen! Especially someone who has battled their demons walked through the zombies in a parade and celebrating themselves!

Almost twenty years ago, my wedding to "Prince Charming," the love of my life, was called off just six days before we were to be married. We were building a house. My oldest son, whose father drowned at twenty-seven, was going to have a dad! My happily-ever- after was finally happening until it wasn't. I could have let this devastate me. Everyone would have understood if I went and curled up on my couch and didn't ever get up. But I didn't. I walked in faith and threw a party.

I called it "The Broken Heart Ball," and I invited anyone who was ever broken-hearted. Hundreds of folks attended. They brought me chocolate and gifts; we laughed and danced the night away. I walked in faith even with my broken heart. The craziest thing happened. People all over the world heard about 'The Broken Heart Ball.' I was flown to New York and featured on *Good Morning America, Inside Edition,* and *CNN.* My faith made me a beacon of hope and positivity to people everywhere. Even with a broken heart and being a jilted bride, I could still walk in faith.

That same "no matter what happens, I am just going to keep walking in faith" mindset built my business. It wasn't some fantastic energy boost of confidence. It wasn't experience or self-confidence. It was my small mustard seed walk in faith that kept me going. Just keep going, no angst, no drama, no rejection could stop me, no ill vibes on whoever caused me anguish, betrayed me or attempted to talk me out of my goals.

Below, you will find a plethora of examples of my walking forward in faith to build a multi-seven-figure business empire.

When my friends wouldn't have a party:
I could have quit; however, I walked forward in faith!

When my oldest son disappeared:
I could have quit; however, I walked forward in faith!

When my personal sponsor ignored my calls, texts, emails:
I could have quit; however, I walked forward in faith!

When people unfriended me:
I could have quit; however, I walked forward in faith!

When I called my best friend of 25 years and told him about my success, and he laughed at me:

I could have quit; however, I walked forward in faith!

When I did events with no attendees:
I could have quit; however, I walked forward in faith!

When people said "no,":
I could have quit; however, I walked forward in faith!

When my phone got shut off:
I could have quit; however, I walked forward in faith!

When I didn't hit rank:
I could have quit; however, I walked forward in faith!

When I didn't understand the compensation plan:
I could have quit; however, I walked forward in faith!

When it got hard:
I could have quit; however, I walked forward in faith!

When I did a Facebook party and didn't make any sales:
I could have quit; however, I walked forward in faith!

When my boyfriend broke up with me:
I could have quit; however, I walked forward in faith!

When my house was in foreclosure:
I could have quit; however, I walked forward in faith!

When people made fun of me:
I could have quit; however, I walked forward in faith!

When I was lonely:
I could have quit; however, I walked forward in faith!

When I was depressed:
I could have quit; however, I walked forward in faith!

When I was sick:
I could have quit; however, I walked forward in faith!

When my son was still estranged for the 8th year:
I could have quit; however, I walked forward in faith!

I did not quit. I didn't give up, and I kept walking forward in faith. I just keep telling myself, "You must choose faith over everything & star in your own life!"

I just keep parading and celebrating with those who come along! Do you want it bad enough to parade? Do you understand faith is a choice and the step that will help you crush your goals? Faith - walking in faith. That's the secret you are looking for, and me, Miss Marilyn, once self-believed to be God's practical joke, is having a love affair with living. I took this walk in faith to write this chapter for you. I have faith (see what I just did there) that you are inspired to parade through your life after reading my words! You, my friend, are made to be the star of your life! You are here to do more. I have given you a mustard seed, and I can't wait to see what you will do with it.

And...
Get a mustard seed.
Use the pens.
Tell your story.
Pitch your opportunity.
Get the trophy.
Buy the building.
Do it all, terrified.
Celebrate yourself!
Star in your own life!
Never quit!
Walk in faith!
I dare you!

May your days be filled with gigantic dreams and faith!

All my love to you and your families,
Miss Marilyn

Coach's Notes:

*Miss Marilyn is the definition of **grit**. Many studies have shown that **grit** is the single most important indicator of success. Everyone will have excuses and setbacks, and everyone will have limiting beliefs and reasons not to succeed. But, Miss Marilyn kept pushing forward. She kept focusing on **progress**. You will still have those hard days, but remember stories like these to inspire you to stay committed to your goals and dreams. Have **faith**.*

MEGAN RUTH BOND

Achievements:

- National Board certificated elementary teacher
- Lives in Southeastern Kentucky with her husband and two children
- Joined the social selling world in 2017
- Hit the top ranks in the network marketing companies she's worked in
- Holds Top Sponsor and Top Seller titles in both network marketing companies
- Became a six-figure earner in her first sixty days of social selling
- Actively works alongside her husband, pastoring a church and organizing community youth events
- Speaker, company trainer, and haymaker

Quote:

**"Be humble, Be hungry, and always
Be the hardest worker in the room."**

- Megan Bond

Coach's Notes:

One of the oldest clichés in network marketing is "facts tell, stories sell." It is a timeless principle. Pay attention to the top leaders in all different network marketing companies. Almost every single one of them has learned how to tell a story. This overwhelmed me at first because I was downright awful at telling stories. I couldn't remember the details. I felt uncomfortable being animated, so I was monotone boring = the boring that puts you to sleep. I was so bad that I completely bombed on my first conference call, where I had the opportunity to speak to a few thousand people. I had only been in network marketing for three weeks. I gave a few stories to the conference call audience, and afterward, my million-dollar mentor said, "On a scale of 1 to 10, you were a 1. You were so boring you sounded like you were at your Father's Funeral." Wow! That was some brutal feedback. It took me years to become good at storytelling. This section is another section I wish I had read before I first started. Thanks, Megan, for laying it out for us.

It doesn't have to be complicated

So often, people are complicating social media. They start to think they need to listen to all the experts, read all the tips, and take an advanced Ph.D. course in social media before they start using it. That is just not true. You have a free space that you can start using very simply today that can help you boost your personal volume and sponsorship in network marketing.

There are three ways you can start to post stories and highlights today that can boost your business. Before I share these with you, I want you to think about your commitment to what I will share. Don't read this chapter as just another tip. Read this chapter with the intention to post right now! Not tomorrow, not next week. I want you to go and use one of these three points as soon as you're done reading this chapter. Do we have a deal? Until you can say yes, don't read ahead! Good, now let's get down to business so you can get more business!

The reality star

Remember how intriguing watching your very first reality show was? For me, it was Survivor on CBS. It was enthralling to meet cast members from the very beginning and connect with them. I was instantly drawn to learning about where they were from and what they did for a living. If I had visited their area or the cast members were from the same state, it made it more interesting.

The cast members would also share their occupations and some info on their lives. The first several episodes were all about making a personal connection to the cast members so that we, as the audience, would want to follow along with their story on the show. Throughout the show, we would learn to like, love, distrust, and even hate cast members based on the shared stories. The show was very addictive.

I got so into it that I would connect cast members' personalities and experiences with people I would personally know. I want to see how my best friend acted or had quirks like certain cast members. I started to see how one cast member had a similar experience growing up, and I would feel an even deeper connection. As the season went on, we saw them in action and how they would speak their minds, play the game, cry, scheme, and hustle. *Survivor* was such a huge hit that reality TV started popping up on every single channel. Their show was such a hit and wildly successful because fans and viewers connected with those cast members.

Social media stories allow us to do the exact same thing that *Survivor* did for so many of us when it came out. We get the privilege to show up in our network feed and be our own reality stars. The best part is that it is absolutely free, and depending on what platform you are on, you have access to billions of people worldwide. So, roll out the red carpet because here you come!

Woody Allen once said, "Success is 80 percent showing up." In the social media world, this is absolutely true. We can all agree that no one will connect with you, trust you, and eventually want to work with you if you are not making an effort. Social media stories give us the gift of being able to open our front door, let our followers into our lives, and have them get a real glimpse into our reality. This includes our homes, our messes, our projects, our opinions, our wins, etc.

Allowing people to see the real us helps build relationships and connections deeper than anything we could do on a website, lead magnet, or copy. If we don't trust and connect with our networks, they'll never buy what we're selling.

Here is the mind-blowing part about using stories on social media. Any responses to your stories, your interactions, the polls that people may vote on, or the questions they may answer in your stories go into messenger. This allows you to begin to nurture an authentic conversation about a topic they connected with because of your stories and sharing your reality. You can be starting the process of getting a future teammate or client because you made a story about what you ate for lunch!

The roadmap

Whenever I talk to anyone about using social media to increase their business, they always ask one question, "How?" There is a simple way to start using story elements on social media today that will help you increase your sales and sponsorship.

You can start by using TikTok, Instagram Reels, and Facebook videos. These are easy places to start posting about your life. People try to complicate it and make it hard, but it really is simpler than you're telling yourself. Go back to the reality star example. People don't want to see scripted, put-together people. They want to see you and want to relate to your real life. Stories are just you and your documentation of your day, so there's no excuse for you not to show up daily.

- Here is a roadmap to success as you start to use stories to sell and get people interested in working with you. First, use humor. People who are bored or stressed out or just in a slump use social media to escape, so humor gives them that escape. They want to get away from that stress and boredom. They are trying to pass the time, and they need a little joy. So, if you think you are funny, often laugh, tell jokes, or anything else that brings joy, share it! There are other people out there that will relate and also find joy in it.

- Show them behind the scenes. Do you meal prep? Do you work out? Do you organize your home? Do you have a top-secret project? Are you organizing your jewelry? Are you getting your beach bag ready for your family vacation? These may sound like mundane tasks, but people out there love to see the day-to-day tasks in other people's lives. Share that with people. People love seeing before and after pictures. This is even true for our tasks. If your house is messy, take a pic. Share it, and then share the after pic when it is all clean.

- Be inspirational. Tell your story or someone else's story that can inspire others—brag on a teammate, friend, or co-worker. Share your wins or someone else's wins. Maybe a podcast inspired you that morning, and you want to share your takeaways from the episode. Let other people share that with you. We love connection, and inspiration is one way that people connect. Share what inspired you with others.

- Showcase your lifestyle product. Share what your company has to offer, whether a product, service, or business opportunity. The biggest hiccup here is that people get stuck. Avoid information constipation when you're showcasing your lifestyle. You don't want just to show a bunch of spec sheets or template graphics of what you are selling.

We want people to know that we're grateful, or we want people to know that we're grateful for our company, for our products, and for what network marketing business has helped us create. You can share some teaching about your product, but make sure it isn't information overload. Keep your sharing helpful. Do before and after DIYs and avoid talking to people. Over-deliver by showing.

- Share content, add other content to your stories. If you have a significant influence with many followers that you are friends with, share their content if it inspires you. Don't be afraid to share those people's content in your stories because more people will connect with something that you might think is funny or inspirational. People will remember that you were the one who shared this super funny video of the person with the pod face wrap. People get to know you and want to follow you because you find great content and share it with your audience.

- Share stories in stories. People remember things twenty times better in a story. Think about a kid's bedtime story. I'm sure you're thinking of a story from your childhood right now or something you were told as a child. Books, movies, and even songs are told as stories. People remember actual stories, so if something happened to you throughout the day, and you're decompressing in your bedroom, tell people the story. People will listen and stick around for your story time.

- Spread excitement around announcements. If you have a new product coming out, you have an event coming up, promo, discount code, or something else going on, share it. People love to get excited when you are excited. Do a short clip of yourself talking about the exciting announcement. Share how you will be launching, using, or interacting with the announcement.

- Business tips. If you are someone on social media selling, and you have a business, people will follow you if they like what they see. Share mindset tips, sales hacks, how to close, how to attract people to your business. Be open to sharing what is working for you. This shows people that you are someone that they can trust. Recommend your favorite podcast, share your music playlist, give people a list of your favorite products. Those are the things that people will take away, and you're adding value to their businesses.

- ***Add captions***. I can't emphasize this enough. On all your videos, you need to be adding captions. Often people are scrolling and consuming social media in places that they can't have the volume turned up. They are at work, lying in bed next to a sleeping spouse, or in a public area. Many people are scrolling past your video because there are no captions to read on the video. You should take the time and use captions. We are looking for quality over quantity. Spend the time to get captions, and don't leave your audience hanging without something to read. I promise you, people will stop and read through the caption to your video, but if there is no caption, you are getting a swift swipe.

- Use your F words. No, this is not what you think! You are not going to feel like posting every single day. I get that. I have those days too. However, you can attract the masses even when you don't feel like posting using F words. Here is a list of F words that you can use when you do not feel the social media vibe. I recommend that you fill your stories with five to ten stories per day.

> Faith

Share about your faith and beliefs.

> Family

Share about kids, spouse, partners, get-togethers, family events.

> Food

Share all food. Meal prep, restaurant visits, and backyard BBQs.

> Fitness

Share your workout, where you work out, and what you wear.

> Friendship

Share your friendship and who lights you up - this can be experiences, jokes, etc.

> Fur babies

Share your cute fur babies and what their days look like—nothing like connecting over your pets. People love animals.

> Fingers

I know it sounds weird, but people love seeing your hands. Show your manicure, your rings, your fingers intertwined, fingers moving, and anything else, including your fingers.

➢ Face

People want to see your face - people connect way more to you than they do to a stock photo.

➢ Feet

Where are your feet taking you? Take a pic on the beach, lying down, etc.

➢ Frugal Thoughts

People love seeing deals. If you are a thrifter, coupon clipper, or mad-dash deal shopper, show people what you got.

➢ Fired Up

Share when you are fired up about something. People love seeing other people experience the zeal of life. Share it!

➢ FOMO

Share when you are missing out. We connect over shared missed experiences. If you were supposed to be at a girls' night, but you missed it, share that!

➢ Favors

Share special company awards, incentive trips, team gifts, etc. People love a good party favor, and they love to see you get spoiled! You can even give the person or company a little shout-out!

➢ Fortune

Share the blessings that you have received. You can humbly do this, but people want to celebrate with you, so share your good fortune.

> ➤ Freedom

Share the freedom you have gained from doing your social selling or your direct sales job at home, especially through COVID, and how you're able to continue those relationships.

> ➤ Failures

Funnily share your last failures. Maybe you burnt your finger or the toast. Maybe you broke something, spilled something, or maybe you made a complete mess. People love seeing failures to see you are human. Show people that your life is not perfect. Show people that you are a messy person.

> ➤ Favorites

Share with people your favorite products. They love to see the unboxing of new products. I love to see you using something for the first time your favorite shirts, your favorite bottoms, your favorite earrings, and then you can tag businesses and people that have, you know, you bought from, and that will make them share those blurbs on their stories and get you more exposure

Coach's Notes:

Megan just dropped some massive wisdom bombs! You now have a roadmap for stories that you can continue to come back to over and over again. The best part is Megan teaches you just to be you while giving you ideas to continue to improve your storytelling. Find ways to always share stories!

MELISSA HARTMANN

Achievements:

- Organization of over 12,000

- Half a million in sales monthly

- Spoke on stage at *Most Powerful Women* in network marketing

Quote:

"God is within her; she will not fall."

- Psalms 46:5

Coach's Notes:

Social media has changed everything! And even still, so many people feel overwhelmed, not knowing what to talk about or how to generate leads genuinely. This specific topic is always one of my most requested topics. Although I teach it consistently, I am always learning. I learned a ton from Melissa in this chapter. I absolutely loved her communication style and the way she broke things down.

Your most underutilized asset

Social media is one of the most underutilized assets in network marketing when people start to grow their businesses. When I ask people why they aren't using their social media to promote their business and products, I have heard every excuse in the book. People tell me they don't have enough followers. They don't have anyone interested, or they don't want their friends and family to think they are weird. I also have people say that they don't know how social media works or it becomes too much work.

I am going to give you the exact social media strategy that anyone can use. It doesn't matter if you have two hundred followers or two thousand. Part of doing social media well is having an intentional schedule. We all have had those friends that start something, and every single post is "Buy this! Buy this!" People lose interest if we only post about our product all the time. You have got to remember that social media isn't just about your content. It is also about being social. That means engaging and creating content that people find engaging.

I have created a plan that has proven to keep your audience engaged and helps you not go crazy trying to figure out what you should be posting. First, decide how many posts you would like to make. You can post several a day or once a day. It doesn't matter as long as you stay consistent. So right now, take a second and decide how many times you want to post and commit to staying consistent.

Now here comes the fun part! You will post about four simple things. That's it! You can cycle through these four things as many times as you have decided to post. I see people all the time try to complicate this system. Don't do it! You want to keep social media simple because it can become a *huge* piece of your business.

So here are the four things you will post about: 1. You. 2. Your dreams. 3. Lessons you have learned. 4. Your company and product. That's it! You really can keep it this simple and create a tremendous following. So, let's break this down and show you how to put it into action.

Pull out a piece of paper right now. We are going to do a quick writing exercise. At the top of the paper, put the four topics across the top. Now take one minute for each column and write everything you can in the one minute about the topic. For example, I can write all the lessons I have learned in my lifetime, "Be true to you. Boundaries need to be set in place, etc." Write whatever comes to mind! You will be surprised how much you can come up with in one or two minutes for each category.

After you have done that, you now have a jumping-off point for creating a content calendar. Go back up and see what you decided to commit to. It may say, "Once a day, five days a week on Instagram," or "Three posts a day on Facebook every day." You can now use your topics and create the calendar for what day you will post what. Keep it simple: Day one: about me. Day two: dreams. Day three: lessons. Day four: company. **Repeat!**

After you have chosen when you want to post, we want to decide how you will keep your audience engaging with you. This simple solution is what I teach our team to keep their posts fun, consistent, and engaging. Every post is a different topic, and as you rotate, you do a couple of things. First, you keep it fresh; second, you educate your audience; third, you create a place to engage and be authentic.

I have seen network marketers make the cardinal mistake of making every single post about buying a product. Stop it. No one is going to follow or listen to you if you keep throwing products at them. When you can follow this simple plan, you keep it interesting. Some of my most engaging posts haven't been about the company. They have been about the lessons I have learned throughout my life.

You are the one that needs to decide how much you post, and like I said before. It doesn't matter what you choose. It matters that you stay consistent. I love this system because it helps the shy sharer have a consistent schedule for posting about the company, product, and opportunity. I have seen people be with a company for a year and still not share about it! Don't make the mistake of not letting people know what you have. Don't make the mistake of hiding from others that you have a great product. Sticking to the schedule will help you share and get better at your message through your posts.

Here is one example of what you can do. I love when Facebook memories pop up. I share lessons from those in my post and talk about the lessons I learned from that time in my life. I love showing people where I was and where I am now. This is such a perfect chance to share, "Hey, look where I was! Here is what I have learned since then. OR here is what I would have told my past self at that time." Facebook memories can be a crucial key to your business when you use them correctly. I know for me, when I look back twelve years ago, I was so disappointed in my life, and I was posting these very vague passive-aggressive posts. I was sucked into the drama and validation of comments like, "OMG, who hurt you?" and "Hope you are okay." It is crazy to me that is where I was in my life. But, instead of just seeing the Facebook memory and keeping all of this to myself, I share the lessons I've taken away since then. I use it as a teaching lesson in my life that I can tell others about and hopefully make an impact on them. When you share experiences and lessons from your heart, it will connect with someone on a deeper level.

Another example is sharing testimonials of people that you have helped with the product or opportunity. You could also share any special announcements that your company has just come out with or share about how the company and product have helped change your life. Unfortunately, I see that people get overwhelmed when it comes to posting about the product.

Most of this isn't because you don't know what to post. Posting is simple! Most of this comes down to mindset about what *you* think about posting. Gary Vee has a book called "Jab Jab, Jab, Right Hook." He means that we are posting content that is fun and interesting, and then we hit them with the right hook, the offer. That is what you are doing with this simple posting schedule. You are doing jabs every time you post about yourself, your lessons, and your dreams. The right hook is the product, offer, and company information. One tip: make sure your right hook has a call to action! Don't just post a testimonial with no call to action. That is what we like to call a right hook that didn't land. Always have a call to action with your right hook. It can be "Comment below to Book a call, get a trial pack," etc.

Now that you have a simple social media schedule and have committed to a scheduling calendar and staying consistent let's talk about engagement. Engagement on every single page, person, community ebbs and flows. It's the nature of social media. Just because you had a ton of engagement this week doesn't mean it is a done deal for the rest of time. Part of engagement has to do with you, and part of it has to do with the algorithm. This means that it is partially out of your control, but don't let this discourage you. You should constantly be evaluating your engagement.

Set aside time each week to check in for ten minutes and see how your posts did this week. Ask yourself, "What posts did well?" "What posts could be improved?" "What does the trend of engagement look like for me?" You will find that you may have one post that is hot and active. Keep engaged with that post. Reply to people's comments, love their comments, bring it back up to your stories, so more people find it engaging.

You must gain insight into your current audience and see what they like to know from you. Please note this does *not* mean that you stop following the schedule. You may find that your product posts have the lowest engagement. That is okay, don't stop posting. Instead, you adjust and tweak to see how you can get more attention.

> **Coach's Notes:**
>
> *This last paragraph may be the most important one in this whole chapter. Why? Too many of us are on* **scroll patrol***. We are on social media without a purpose, and we scroll for hours without any efficiency. We get easily distracted. By setting aside focus time, you will get so much done in such a short amount of time. By making time to assess your social media, you will be able to become more effective continually. Here is what I did for three years to dial in my message because, at first, no one engaged with my content on social media. Every month I would look at my top five posts and my bottom five posts. Then I would make observations about the commonalities of each. With time, I learned what my audience resonated with about me. It never became a different version of it. Every post was mine, of course. I just gained insights into where I best connected with others. Each of you is different, but by doing this self-assessment monthly, you will make constant progress!*

Learn the craft

One of my team members reached out to me recently and said, "I have a hard time talking about my dreams with other people. I am not used to talking about myself." Do any of you struggle with this too? I know we don't talk about our dreams enough, and I want to share with you the advice I gave this team member. First, start dreaming. Create vision boards, think about what type of life you want to live. Don't hold back. Next, remind yourself that there are other people out there that want to dream too. These people will connect with you based on what you're sharing. Finally, remind yourself that God has put this dream and these people into your life for a reason. Your job is to connect the two and be a help to them.

If this seems scary, start small. Start by sharing your dreams with one person. Your upline or someone in network marketing is a great start. We are an industry full of dreamers! They will understand. You can even start and tell them that you are nervous about sharing. Another tip is that you could post in your group and have others hold you accountable. Tell them, "I am posting for the first time, and I am scared! I will report back tonight." Use the resources you have around you to be a built-in support system for you.

I am always blown away by the stories our team shares with me when they start using this system and share about themselves, the lessons they have learned, their dreams, and the business. For example, I had one person tell me that she had no idea how many people were reading her posts until people started messaging her and telling her what an inspiration she was to them.

Learning the craft of posting takes time. Give yourself the gift of figuring it out, playing around with it, and being curious about how you like to post and engage on social media. I shared with you how I figured out I love to use Facebook memories. That came through experimenting and crafting my message. Even now, I still feel like I have so much to learn. I have been consistently posting on Facebook and Instagram daily for two and a half years, and I have come a long way, but I can't wait to see what my posts look like in two more years. What's great is that eventually, when you can look at your memories and say, "Oh my gosh, a year ago

I had this great caption, I can save that to my notes. I can recycle that content and send it over to Instagram, or send it over to and make it into a TikTok or Reel." You're going to have consistently abundant content because you're always creating it!

There are several different platforms to use for social media. In this day and age, I think it is essential to use at least two platforms. Every single platform has different strengths, and each one has a diverse audience. So, I came up with a way to remember to post on various platforms.

Here is a phrase to remember, "You want to get **FIT** every single day!" To keep your body healthy and strong, you have to stay fit and active. To keep your business healthy and strong, you have to keep active on FIT. FIT stands for Facebook, Instagram, and TikTok. These are the platforms that I have decided to use. This acronym has helped our team remember that staying active on social media is crucial to our businesses.

You can use whatever platform you like. Maybe you are going to stay LIT (LinkedIn, Instagram, TikTok). It doesn't matter what platforms you use. What matters is consistency! I have said it before, and I will say it again: stay consistent on whatever platforms you decide to engage on.

Once you decide what platforms you are using, you will start to get in a rhythm of posting. Maybe you will post on Facebook at 7:00 am, Instagram at 10:00 am Facebook at noon, TikTok at 2:00 pm, Facebook at 4:00 pm, TikTok at 6:00 pm, and Instagram at 8:00 pm. Does this seem overwhelming? Deep breaths. It really isn't that bad. And if this isn't for you, remember you can automate all of this. There are apps out there that you can set up beforehand, and they will post at the exact times you tell them to on the right platform.

Let's go over some more examples so that you can see how this works across multiple platforms. Let's say I have decided that I want to do product posts on Tuesdays and Thursdays. I have some trial packs that I would like to send to people to try out and make some money by the weekend. So, on Tuesday, I post a testimonial with a call to action at the bottom on Instagram. On Thursday, I post a product post on Facebook about how fantastic the product is, and my call to action is to hit the like button for a chance to get a free trial pack.

Because I have already posted about the product on Instagram on Tuesday, my Thursday post on Instagram will be about something different. Just for fun, I may post a TikTok on Friday showing how I use the product and see how many lives I can change with that video. I have shared my product now three times across three different platforms without overwhelming my audience! Here's the thing guys, your language is everything, so I automatically assume, and I have this thought that one of them is really going to hit.

Like I mentioned before, part of the plan for all of this is working on your mindset around posting. One of my favorite things to tell myself once I posted is, "This is going to be well received. The exact right people will see this." What you believe becomes your reality. If you are thinking, "No one is going to bite," that will become true. Start believing that you are going to get comments galore. Start believing that you are sharing a life-changing product. Start believing that you will make sales on social media.

I have a couple more tips for you. First, it doesn't matter how many followers you have. Be consistent. Second, stop overthinking it. This system that I shared is easy. Remember that it takes time to get your voice and figure out how you want to post. Keep it simple. Third, follow up on social media. If people comment, make sure you comment back. If they message you, message them back. Social media is supposed to be social!

One of the most beautiful things about social media is the opportunity it gives us. Social media gives every single person a chance to connect with people around the world. Different platforms give us different ways of engaging and expressing ourselves. Some of you are going to love Facebook. I know I do. It feels like it is relationship-based. Some of you are going to love TikTok and find fun, creative ways to post videos. Instagram is aesthetically pleasing. You have the opportunity to use all of these to your advantage and build a business around them. You can do endless things with social media, and it all starts with using this system.

You have the opportunity to connect with some of the most incredible people you'll ever meet by posting about yourself, sharing lessons you have learned, dreaming with others, and educating them about your product, company, and opportunity. Don't take that for granted. Start using social media today. You don't need to be more prepared, have more experience, or have a better message. You just need to start sharing. Do the work that I gave you at the beginning of this chapter, and you are on your way to creating massive success in network marketing.

Coach's Notes:

As Melissa said, "First, it doesn't matter how many followers you have. Be consistent. Second, stop overthinking it." Start posting consistently now! Keep coming back to this chapter to refine your messaging. Rinse and repeat!

NINA SALKIC

Achievements:

- Mom of four kids

- Bachelor of Social work and Master of Political sciences

- Couldn't find a job in her little society, so she found inspiration and a way to help people and complimented her life calling in network marketing

- She was instrumental, and the main reason her country Bosnia and Herzegovina was opened to network marketing and hit a six-figure earner in the first year

- She quickly built a team of 30,000 people and has done millions of dollars in sales volume from a country with only three million people

- Her international team is in: Balkan countries, Germany, Austria, Switzerland, Sweden, Norway, USA, Portugal, Italy, and she is building a team in Ghana, Africa.

- Nina is #1 in her company for product knowledge, getting customers, and helping others to do the same

Quote:
"Share your knowledge. It is a way to achieve immortality."

Nina's Story

Mastering the art of educating your partners

Many of us are employed or have our own businesses in ways that serve us. It helps us pay for things, survive and buy services and goods that help create comfort, experience, entertainment.

I often say money is a "blessing tool" that allows us to afford the essentials and be "God's wallet" for helping others and open up the world's possibilities in the present.

Money as our focus can be either a goal or the meaning of our happiness.

Our work commitment and success will be reflected by how much we allow ourselves to earn. Of course, our focus and how we are programmed since childhood about money will also play a part, but these are secondary factors.

We have all heard hundreds of stories of successful people running corporations, hotels, restaurants, or starting some type of their own successful businesses. We listened to videos about their path to prosperity and were amazed at their *loop* and the audacity to prioritize their drive to succeed.

As much as we have heard and seen other people do this, very few of us learn the lesson given to us all the time: *you can do it too.* Our subconscious, however, overpowers our mind and circulates with every attempt to accomplish something great for us. We simply do not see ourselves as such and usually find hundreds of excuses for our vulnerability and as a result, our mind focuses on the wrong things. Here are some examples of where we get stuck:

- I don't have enough money
- I don't have enough education

- I don't have enough acquaintances
- I don't have enough ideas
- My circumstances are different
- My work organization does not provide enough options

But, but, but! We focus our minds on lack, scarcity, and fear. All around us we have abundance, and all we see is a lack.

There is an opportunity that exceeds all formal businesses where we can express ourselves.

Network marketing.

Networking is the enlightened path to social, material, and mental well-being. We can experience the freedom of doing business, choices to work the way we would want to work, have an international action and stamp ourselves, duplicate, on to like-minded people.

It sounds hard to believe that we can make such choices by summing up our life circumstances. We grew up in the matrix of imposed values and rules that are placed on us for generations...

To have a social impact, we need to follow the protocol of society, right? To belong to something, to limit oneself to something.

Most of our ancestors did not find opportunities to emphasize their values and pass them on to generations of people the same way we now enjoy but there have always been a few initiators who wanted to convey their constructive ideas through these limiting social gatherings. Have you ever thought about how someone in the past who had a social influence, someone who left a mark on humanity in science, technology-actually managed to reach the depths of the human soul?

He DARED just like those of individuals mentioned at the beginning.

They had such a strong *desire* to make it happen. They considered what was born as an idea in their subconscious mind so crucial for human existence, that it overcame the zone of comfort and sufficiency and excuses. Many people as a part of network marketing industry, unfortunately, professionally and skillfully pack it into defeats of unpreparedness and immaturity to perform.

Coach's Notes:

Let's give even more perspective on Nina's incredible story. In her home country of Bosnia, the average person makes almost $7,000 USD annually! It would have been easy for her to create every excuse for her not to succeed in her country, but she broke through those limiting beliefs. As she mentioned, she never focused on the lack of abundance, but instead, she focused on the opportunity. We all have challenges. We also all have opportunities. It is your choice on what you focus your mind on.

Today's leader

In addition to our own company, we monitor many successful networkers at organized network marketing events and follow them through social networks to learn from them.

We love following people to figure out how they operate, partially wishing to copy and implement what is going well in their businesses. We love seeing their motivational messages, strategies, business advice, and how they lead their teams. It is so inspiring to see how many people willingly share how to be successful in network marketing by showing the "behind the scene" view of how to operate.

The bravest ones who intimately share what growing a network marketing business looks like are also those who have immense popularity and viewership on social platforms right?

They have *dared* to find a way to channel their inspiration, they have been followed by people who lack it, and they are reluctant to turn such ideas into a verbal equivalent. Simple.

Imagine how selfless these people are, that they have managed to overcome all those barriers you are working on skillfully to cultivate in yourself. Their mission is bigger than their ego, which in many cases scares you with the fear to get you out of your own way.

Imagine the size of a leader who is willing to fight with the thoughts that you may have, too. You are letting those thoughts stop you, but the actual leaders overcome them. That same leader serves not only his team but such a large community of network marketers.

Now stop for a second and think about this: Shouldn't we actually all be supporting each other? How do you categorize the meaning of a "team" if you do not stand out and contribute to the community you grow at least in your private team space? Being a true leader means contributing to the whole.

Coach's Notes:

*What a reverse way of thinking! Nina talks about how **selfless** the people who crush social media are. Frequently many people feel uncomfortable wanting to promote their ideas on social media. Nina gives a unique observation on the fears we have to overcome to put ourselves out there. So let me continue with that thought. Stop being **selfish**! Stop avoiding using your talents because you are worried about what others may think of you. Stop allowing the opinion of others to prevent you from going after your dreams.*

It is all our responsibility

We invite partners from our organization to listen and follow *them* because the zone of sufficiency and comfort blocks our ability to step out and take control, which is realistically the recipe for our secretly desired success! We feel that it is easier for someone else to do this passionate public work better than ourselves.

I am a company partner, and when the idea for starting a company was shouldered onto me, it would have been easy to pass it off to someone else. It was not easy to open a company in a network marketing uneducated society. Where I come from, network marketing was very strange, and it was a challenge to explain how the "doing" of this business has to be made. It was hard.

It would have been easier to say "no" and do something simple with smaller efforts, be employed and stay classy.

But I realized that this seemingly more complex way is the best and only way to grow into a prosperous person and have the thriving business of my dreams. I broke down all my own prejudices about the industry, because there were no other prejudices than mine. I realized that my community, my growing team, needed someone like me. And if I don't, who will? That is what we ask for: all of our prospects get over themselves, their blocks and fears and join network marketing in its calling to change the way people do business.

While we don't hear the applause of the audience gathering on the stage of our success, that doesn't mean we don't have their attention and don't look at what we're doing along the way.

Although painful for the ego, I realized that so many people enable, make happy, cheer up, channel vital information, instill hope in *others,* and do not focus on that "poor self" who lost course in everything and waited for it to fall from the sky. My success began to sprout from the seeds I planted as a sign of good. Because of the good we are all here, the policy of the network marketing industry is conceived on these postulates. Like it or not, this industry wakes up even the sleepiest people - only if it has a higher dimension that allows themselves to be awakened.

Leading from the front

When I decided to grow my business, my team grew automatically. I felt a responsibility to teach and help grow new leaders. I created something that would be out of formality for my team. Something that isn't reduced to just a written word in groups, a brief notice, back-office training, or a classic opportunity presentation. This would be something different.

I was inspired. I wanted this to be something that felt like a family gathering. I resonated to frame my leadership vocation towards helping people learn not to run away from problems and learn the steps of looking fear in the eyes. This isn't a skill that was going just to serve them in network marketing. It is a skill that, if mastered, could change every single area in their lives and have them show up for themselves, their families, and the community entirely differently!

Since I wanted a big challenge, one that would move myself from the heels and leave an impression on others, only those willing to follow me and participate in it were actually able to participate. With that, I managed to filter people who are, according to the book *GoPro*: willing, coachable, and hungry. This helped me keep showing up, keeping my word, and going all-in on a fully committed group to change. I got an *aha* moment as Ramadan was approaching.

Ramadan in the Muslim world is the Holy Month of Fasting, mercy, forgiveness, cleansing of body, mind and soul, and lasts 30 days. The greatest experience I could set for myself, and I made the mind work for me without pre-prepared content. After a daily fast of food and drink that lasted about 15 hours, exhausted body but fed and motivated soul, over 100 of us were connected in the wee hours of the night and were consistent with our desire to grow. We did the deep work to prepare ourselves for what would come next in our business.

Formal exit from the comfort zone

Team support is the holy grail of business. Only a leader can produce leaders. Everything we do is duplicated to the rest of the team. Team will surely follow you if you show that you will be the first to do a certain task.

What is the point? Be the first. Be a mover. Fall in front of everyone, but at least try. Don't overthink, act! You are familiar with the saying: "Say yes, then figure out how"? This sentence changed my view of my whole life from the bottom up. And I believe it will work for you this way too. I practiced it in business and the private field, on the most ordinary little things- when I am too lazy to do some household chores for example. No hesitation and thinking, just go do it, and all the dice will sort themselves out.

It was with the team of partners, they educated themselves with what I was preparing " along the way". Why do I say this incidentally? Every day I prepared topics for the same night!

Whenever I gave myself space and time, for someone who is quite disorganized in life (I believe that most of us are like that), I struggled to manage anything. I fall into the abyss of my insecurities and my view of my own imperfection brings me to tears.

In this pressure way, I didn't give myself the time or the chance to start analyzing anything - and in the excitement and short time I gave myself, it turned out the way I could only imagine it to be. I pressed my mind to work for me. Not the opposite.

Many successful people have stated the same and recognized "working under their own pressure" as the basis of success. At any moment they were ready for interviews, webinars, and training that was done masterfully. Right now, I want you to do a self-evaluation. Are you ready to work under pressure? Could you give a fast interview? Present a webinar right now? Do training for your company? If the answer is no, it is time to get yourself ready.

Here are several areas where you can help yourself prepare. The *three dimensions* of education are the basis of every coaching. Let's take a look at each of them:

1. Mindset

2. Skillset

3. Strategy

Mindset is working on yourself and your worldview, open thinking, and accepting the diversity of human choices. It is the topic on which the volumes of the books have been written. I think that there is no unprocessed topic or education in this field. We are witnessing how much there is a demand for it globally - not only for networking but in general in the private and business world.

It is the part of us that has been closed for generations- the wisdom of our consciousness and connection with the natural that we instinctively want to be. This is because we have reached the automation threshold in a society that is increasingly losing its meaning of existence. The feeling of our own satisfaction and fulfillment, acceptance of ourselves and who we are, that there is a place for each of us in the world and that our voice should be heard - is the least we can do for ourselves through education.

The modern system is not supported by a free man but by one who obeys the system imposed on us and creates an army of followers through political, religious, and national ideologies. Therefore, revealing lesser-known secrets and how certain people throughout history have reached inner beings closest to their Creator will bless you and your life. It will also open a different perspective on the world to many people on your team.

You are not even aware of how much you will improve an individual's quality of life and help them be better spouses, parents, and children of their parents. How much acceptance will reign in the team, the built friendship, the sense of belonging... How many walls will you tear down, and what culture will you build to give fuel to their ambitious cells. Read books every single day and pass it on to your people through thematic educations- because they will read books through you without knowing it while you educate them, even though they may not like reading.

After working on yourself, apply it to business.

Skillset is a podium that opens the door to skills that will help represent and brand yourself more effectively as a person and partner of the company. My people, this is a netWORK marketing industry that people enter. As in any work organization, teach them *how* to work. We expect too much from the people on our team. People are lost in the sea of information. They have entered with the desire to change themselves, their world, and the world of others for the better.

The Holy Qur'an states: "God will not change the state of a nation until they change themselves"" (Ar-Raad, 11). Wasn't everything told to us? We cannot influence change until we provoke a desire for change in people and guide them to make it happen.

How many of us knew all the information about our company's products and services in the beginning? Nobody. How many of us knew how to recommend a product and sell it properly? Nobody.

How many knew how to separate business from the classic sales model and how to connect with people without looking like a sales cliché? Nobody.

How many of us knew how to present ourselves from day one and come out confident in public? Nobody.

We learn about these things. We are not coming ready for them. If networking was an easy job, do you think it would be this successful and exciting, colorful, and would have so many haters? That's what I'm telling you. Appreciate the boon of knowing this business because it is reserved for special people.

Strategies aim to achieve a specific goal that needs to be planned after adopting the first two dimensions of coaching. You need to understand that these three parts are inseparable and that it is pointless to move with strategies until the mind is open and the skills are learned that you will later strategically turn into the goal.

You don't become an entrepreneur overnight, and this is the part where you set realistic frameworks for achieving the goal and what they need to achieve it.

Everyone is in a hurry to achieve something: big money, social position (rank), influence, skills, presentation skills, etc.

"Be quick but not hurry"

– John Wooden

Know that he who stares is always late. Before each start of a collaboration, put into practice to define what your partners want to do and how you will influence them if this initial motivation weakens them. Always know what you are up to with people and refresh your wishes after each small goal is made. The more minor victories you make, the more appetites will grow as people become aware of the success.

- Abilities that will emerge from their hidden ambitions
- The values they will realize after realizing the prison in which they lived

- Opportunities that open up to them by expanding their horizons

- Their acceptance - as persons worth reaching the rank, money, and everything that network marketing brings them indulge because, in principle, all things are very simple, only we complicate them ourselves due to ignorance, lack of experience, or fear of the unknown.

Remember that your success will not be diminished by the inability of others to recognize your value because your value as a leader is a feeling created inside. It is easy to express if you give them that opportunity.

No singer, actor, or anyone you can imagine had a pre-formed audience waiting for him, but they created the circumstances that brought him the audience with his works and art. It is up to you to dare, learn and seek knowledge, duplicate all the knowledge with your team through education - and finally enjoy what you leave for generations of people as a trace of your life.

Coach's Notes:

All principles are simple! When you can simplify your success to focusing on the mindset first, everything begins to change. Mindset will eat skills and strategies for breakfast. It isn't to say that the skills or strategies aren't essential, but you will not truly implement them without the right mindset. With the right mindset, your ability to learn the skills and strategies will greatly increase. Get out of your own way. Sometimes we can overcomplicate everything by doubting ourselves. We doubt our approach, follow up and close. We doubt our social media posts. Stop it! Get out of your own way. Do your best and forget the rest.

SHYLO ECKSTROM

- 7-figure network marketer
- Featured in *Success From Home*
- Rebel Millionaire

Quote:
Imperfection is beauty, madness is genius, and it's better to be absolutely ridiculous than absolutely boring."

- Marilyn Monroe

Master your habits and master your life. Find balance and crush your days!

Life can be challenging for all of us. Throw in a lot of hard work, and it will get even more challenging. But life doesn't always have to be unbalanced. Sure, some days you're going to feel out of whack - and that's completely okay - and some days you're going to feel resilient as hell! That is how this life works, but people get stuck in the rut of the grind, *or* they feel unsatisfied chasing the unachievable "balanced" life. You will never always be balanced, but you can do things today to help yourself get to a better place and use that energy to move your business forward.

Coach's Notes:

I have seen Shylo have success in multiple companies. I have seen her highs and her lows. I know she speaks from experience. I wish I had the advice you are about to receive. After two and a half years in network marketing, I was so burnt out I didn't want to get on my own team calls or attend my own convention. No one gave me a game plan of any type of balance, so I overworked myself to the point of exhaustion. I overworked myself so hard, I was counterproductive. Pay close attention to the following strategies and implement them in your own life.

Grounded and Balanced

I want to give you some motivational tips for how to stay grounded and balanced on the days when you're feeling a bit crazy. Also, give yourself some grace. We all can be shit shows sometimes, and I say embrace your inner *Shit Show*!

You will fail, and you will stumble, but as long as you're not afraid to do it, you will eventually succeed. The most successful people in the world have taken each bump in the road, every mistake, and made it a learning lesson. In reality, there is no such thing as failure unless you quit trying. Every failure is a steppingstone to success. *"Fail forward, do it often and do it fast,"* I quoted myself there.

So how many times you fall isn't what's important. What's important is how many times you get back up and succeed. Be willing to fail. It will help to point you in the right direction. Only look back to grow from the mistakes but do not stay there. We are not going that way. There is no use beating yourself up or staying in the failure. Fail, learn from it, and move on.

Another way to remain balanced is to dedicate some time to yourself. Set aside 10 -15 minutes every day for some *you* time. Whether it be to stretch, take a walk, watch an inspirational video on YouTube (I love Les Brown, Eric Thomas, Brene Brown, and Tony Robbins). Read some quotes or pages from your favorite book (I love The Four Agreements by Don Miguel Ruiz). Anything to start your day with some *balance*.

Try to refrain from hopping on social media when you first wake up. You never know if you're going to see something negative that can determine how your day will flow. It's the same thing with your email. If you are in the practice of starting your day by opening the computer, apps, or phone, *stop it*! Instead, take the first couple of minutes of your day and intentionally do something to connect to yourself and be with yourself.

Another tip is self-motivation. You are the only person who can keep your good vibes flowing and your balance maintained. You are going to be the frontrunner for the whole workday and the background noise in your head. You are constantly growing and learning, so you are the most important thing. Besides, you are the one succeeding, right?

Train yourself to be balanced while the rest of the world throws curveballs at you by saying daily affirmations. Tell yourself good things about yourself throughout your day and when you wake up. I promise it will help your day go smoother!

You're continuously growing and doing a damn good job at it. Remember never to stop raising the bar. Remember that the road will get tough, and things aren't always going to go your way, but if you push through whatever it is that's stopping your flow, your balance will come!

Lastly, if you need constant motivation from an outside source, you shouldn't be an entrepreneur. This is some tough love, but it's true not every day is sunshine and rainbows. You have to be able to have a strong vision and why on the tough days.

Coach's Notes:

*Starting your day the right way makes all of the difference! Shylo gave you simple strategies that will help your business out tremendously. Many things can go wrong in a day, but it is like putting on the armor before a battle when you prepare yourself each morning. It doesn't mean you will always win the battle, but you have a much better chance of it when you're in full armor. Put the armor on every morning. Do personal development. Refrain from social media and keep growing and working on **you**!*

More from Shylo

I just shared some great tips, but let's get into specifics. There are actual things you can do today to change your life and business.

Ask any seven and eight-figure earner about their morning routine, and not only will it blow your mind, it will also reveal why they are where they are! The most successful people in the world all have impeccable habits. What are yours? In any coaching or mentoring call, I first ask someone to seek help or guidance. Tell me about your morning? They usually say things like, "I get up, and the kids get up. It's chaotic. I slam three coffees and..." - you get the picture. I can say without fail that most people asking me for help have little to no good morning habits and feel out of control. Do not stress if this is you. I can help you quickly turn it around but let's assess.

How does your morning start? Take your time to think of this. From the moment you get up for the first two hours. We will be using a similar method to the compound effect to get your habits matching your mentors or greater. F   or those of you that have your day done by 10 am, congrats, and I applaud you. Yes, this is possible, and you can read along to see if you can add or improve any area. I am speaking to those who fly by the seat of our pants, people who everyone in the family avoids in the morning because it's true craziness.

I did my own assessment a few years ago, and I realized at times in my life, when I was most in tune with my habits and stuck to them relentlessly, I was the most fulfilled, but also, my business was on fire.

I will not tell you to go all-in and add fifty things to your morning, but I will ask you to start with a few essential things to shift your whole being. First, turn your phone to silence and turn it face down every night before bed! This is non-negotiable. So why did I start at night? If you do not get enough quality sleep and vibrations and lights constantly wake you, you are already destroying your following day. I will not take no for an answer because this is for your health.

Now we move to the morning. At this point, you got quality rest, or at least you are on the right path. Now what? I love to build from habits, and the second one I challenge everyone with is making your damn bed! It sounds so minor and straightforward so then do it. A few years ago, I went through a very challenging time in my life and business and had slipped out of all my good habits. I was sleeping in my pajamas all day and felt scattered. I knew I had to start a better, healthier routine, but where would I begin? You guessed it. I started making my bed. Obviously, I will encourage you to brush your teeth and such, but these are automatic. Make this one thing your automatic each morning. It also is a big checkmark for those who love checking off our lists. Win-win.

Again, taking a proper inventory of your mornings will help you see the areas you need some help in or add to a healthy habit. I am a supplement gal. I take many supplements in the morning and know many do, or at least you get your coffee in. Set time aside to get that in right away. I also believe in moving your body each day. Now I do not expect you to jump in and start going to cross fit and change your whole world in a day. That is a great way to *not* stick to something. Start daily and weekly with new things. Maybe you add in a twenty min walk right after your vitamins or coffee. I also suggest that you do some body movement and grab your AirPods and turn on motivational training or some sort of positivity to rock your morning. Ahh, that brings me to one more non-negotiable that I already mentioned. *No social media*/phone for the first thirty minutes of your morning at all. The last thing you need the moment you wake up is stressful messages demanding your time and presence. Or conflict resolution at 7 am – *not* happening. I cannot tell you how dramatically my mood and life changed when I did this one thing. Trust me; no one needs you at 5 am on the west coast to walk them through an order. You need to put your mask on first before you can help others, and that is your morning routine. Stick to it and trust me!

Every single one of us is either adding to our days or taking away. You also have to find the things not serving you. I tend to say yes to most things then get overwhelmed. I simply go through my to-do lists and find the things that serve God, my family, or my business. If it doesn't serve that or get me closer to my goals, then I eliminate it. Be able to say no from time to time. Never sacrifice what you are doing for meaning we do not sacrifice kids, family, or moments in time we can't get back. We can, however, sacrifice a night out, that Netflix series, or bottomless mimosas at brunch. Of course, you can reward yourself from time to time; just try to watch the habit of constantly rewarding. I can get in these modes, so I am referring to myself.

I know many of you love lists, so let's make one. First, you already wrote down your morning routine, right? Well, do it now. Let's look at a few things you can add that can help you crush it by 10 am!

- Make your bed

- Get dressed (yes, I know many of you who sit in PJ's all day). Working from home has many perks, but this one helps move your butt

- Get your supplements in

- Morning devotional or motivational. YouTube is your friend; use it!

- Move your body for twenty mins (walking is just as good as anything)

- Audio or a book; try to get in ten minutes of this

- Have kids? Get them going, or your fur babies. Make sure you take care of your family

This needs an explanation. If you have to get other people up, fed, and such, you have to wake up early enough to get your things handled. I started waking up at 5:30 am every day. By 10 am, I had all my work things conquered, and the house was clean and done for the day. If you want to create a life you always wanted, it takes some skills, but it's worth it.

Emails messages, follow-ups, reach outs! Whatever you do for your business, this is the time right now. This is officially your power hour. No distractions for the morning, and you are ready, and now you can use this hour to get the tasks needed for your business. Record videos or do training. Use this time to get it done. Imagine a day that is entirely done by noon! It's possible, but it all starts with *you*.

I do want to have an honorable mention category that is very, very important. You bought this book, so you clearly want to reach your goals, but do you ever take time to just enjoy all the things in life? I mentioned briefly that my life and business hit a tough spot.

I found myself lost, sad, and frustrated with how things were going. I was burnt out! Like really burnt out. I suffered from MLM PTSD (it's a thing). I was stuck. I did not know if I should be a leader any longer and questioned everything. I will tell you this is normal from time to time, and it's what you need to be clear in your vision. All I did was work! Work all day and all night in my PJs. Everything in my life was emotionally based on how work was going! This is also a very unhealthy thing. If I was winning, recruiting had great training, I was so happy. If there was drama, conflict, and things were challenging, I was also going through it in all ways.

My family ebbed and flowed with the business too. If mom was dealing with work, better leave her be. I can't tell you how many events or experiences were shifted because of work. I had to overcome this, so I did. I started to smell the roses! I needed little rewards or escapes that helped me relax, release and rejuvenate. Bottom line, friends, get some hobbies! Sounds simple, right? Well, it's not as easy as that.

I have many friends and colleagues that tell me all they do is work. They love it but also start to feel fried. You have to find joy in life outside of work. Travel, spa days, gardening, whatever it is, maybe just reading a book. Set aside time for it at least weekly. Make sure you budget for certain hobbies. I recommend choosing a free or affordable hobby if you are anything like me - go big or go home. At least that way, you can keep up with the hobby you choose. The last thing I need is people coming to me going broke because they took my advice. Kidding but not really - be smart, please.

By now, you should have a good assessment of your daily and morning habits. Do it if you have not! You should already have a side list of what you would like to add and eventually what your ideal day contains. Put your hobbies in this as well, making sure you have time in the day for fun, family, and faith! It's so important that your day includes everything. If you want a great business, it starts at home with your family, well-being, and overall mental and physical health. You have to get oxygen into your muscles, fresh air in your lungs, and plenty of water and sleep.

Again, I am not telling you to become a bodybuilder, but your physical and mental health are in a relationship. You can't have one without the other.

This brings me to the last part of this chapter. You can do all the things mentioned above, but

it will not matter if you do not identify your *one thing*. Or things that have held you back or hindered you. For years I worked harder, worked out harder, focused on things I could control because my one thing was always in the background. I always liked to have a few drinks. I struggled with social anxiety my whole life. A few glasses of wine and boom, I became fun, social, and relaxed. The reality was it was a monster hiding in the closet. It was always lingering. I wasn't always having fun or having great times. I had many mornings wondering what I said or who I hurt. I called them and felt bad. Alcohol for me was confidence juice or a crutch to get me through unsure times or insecurities. As I was faced with several challenges a few years ago, it completely took me over. I knew that this one thing would hurt my family and business, but I did not know how or who to talk to.

Well, I hit rock bottom, and before I share the rest, I am not saying you have to quit drinking or anything, but we all have something. Food, procrastination, self-sabotage, negative self-talk, porn, well, you get the point. Something is stopping us from being our greatest selves. Before you make all these changes we talked about, you first have to have a meeting in the mirror and get very vulnerable and accountable. Only then will things genuinely change. This also comes down to how much you want it. Change is painful sometimes, but it's part of the process.

Okay, so I fell flat on my damn face. I made a substantial public mistake, and I hurt people. I made an ass of myself but what many did not know was it was the one thing I had prayed for three years. I asked God to help me quit this one thing, and I would serve him and help others. God shows up in interesting ways, but I am proud to say that I am sober and healthy a year later, and my life and business have never been stronger or healthier. I took my sobriety to my platform and found that the little devil on my shoulders is a light for many hiding in the dark and not sure where to go. I am grateful for the hurt, sadness, and lessons as I had to go through it to fully understand what it takes to get to the next level.

We live in a world where we only see the highlight reels. Everyone and everything is filtered. So, I challenge you to be a rebel and be yourself. It sounds easy but can get watered down and filtered out. Be honest with yourself if you are ready to take control of your day, morning, and year. Identify your thing or things, make a list and start making your damn bed.

Coach's Notes:

*If you aren't following a variation of this chapter, don't ask why you aren't having success. It starts with **you**. It starts in the morning, and it starts with the right mindset and habits. You will make mistakes, but if you follow a blueprint similar to this, eventually, these new routines will become habits. In the last fourteen years, I haven't missed one day of prayers or personal development. Not one day! Why? Because I understood the power of habits just like Shylo has. Her success is no fluke. Shylo does the basics better than most and has more success than most.*

SUE BRENCHLEY

Achievements:

- Mom of four and grandma of thirteen
- A thirty-year veteran of network marketing
- Seven-figure annual earner
- Member of Million Dollar Hall of Fame
- Over ten million dollars in career earnings
- Organizations in thirty-three countries and growing

Quote:

"You become what you believe"

- Oprah Winfrey

Sue's Story

Some days I feel like Cinderella. My early years felt like hard work that never amounted to the life that I really wanted to lead. Life felt like I was always looking up at the castle, wishing for more. So how is it possible that I became a network marketing millionaire? Let me tell you the story and the secrets that led to my fairy tale life.

As a baby boomer born in the '50s, and a product of the post-war era, I looked like many people from the outside. But hidden inside my life was a secret. My dad had served in the Korean war, and even after the fighting in the war stopped, he came home and continued to battle, fighting his own demons and wars. This resulted in addictions that led to a life of dysfunction and living below paycheck to paycheck.

My stay-at-home mom battled mental illness and desperately wanted to have a family and live the American dream. But, unfortunately, my family's lives became a merry-go-round of trying to keep up with the Joneses (oh wait, our last name was Jones) and all the disappointments and stress accompanying the road to success. We were a family struggling to move closer to the castle, but we were sad and desperate behind closed doors.

I know that many of you can relate to being the person whose family fought about money, couldn't pay for sports or lessons, and struggled to provide the necessities of life. You might even be in that struggle right now or know someone who is. But the truth is you don't have to repeat the cycle and endure another generation of just getting by. Instead, you can create a new story and even find your happily ever after if you are coachable and have a vehicle and system with the right tools to get started.

Coach's Notes:

Sue is one of the few million dollar annual earners in all of network marketing. She has seen it all and is familiar with everything from the old-school timeless principles to the new modern-day techniques. The principles never change, but the techniques are always adapting. Despite her incredible income, she is continually improving. In the last few months, Sue was at two of my Masterminds. She knows that successful change is inevitable, so she always stays up to date on the latest and greatest techniques. I have had five different lunches with Sue in the last two years, discussing her incredible insights on creating systems that work. I can't wait for you to discover some of her best lessons on making a system work.

Power of 5

If you weren't part of network marketing in the '80s and '90s, it might be difficult to relate to the pre-social media world and why it is relevant to the systems that will work for you today. My first system tools were a green cassette tape and conference calls that cost money. I am passionate about the power of systems and the foundation they provide for long-term duplication and success in your business. I am also convinced that so many more people in our industry could ultimately succeed with better tools and systems, and I'm excited to share some ideas with you. It doesn't matter if your system is sharing an audio cassette or a TikTok video, what is important is committing to the system.

We named our system "The Power of 5" because years ago, we learned that 80 percent of your income would come from three to five of your top producing leaders, and we wanted to keep everything to five steps and five minutes or less to create simplicity and empower people to keep it simple and take actionable steps forward.

As soon as we started to develop this system, we began to see the number five was showing up everywhere. The "five-second rule" with Mel Robbins started a cultural phenomenon of people skipping the snooze button in the morning, and we wanted to simplify the steps for people to take each day in a way that would result in a similar outcome in our business.

At the core or foundation are the five priorities of any business: people, products, purpose, plan, and profits. So many times, I see the focus on products instead of people, and I believe that is a mistake. Although quality products are definitely foundational in the success equation, people can never be discounted as the highest priority. We believe that the profits will follow by focusing on solving people's problems through quality products that impassion people with purpose and providing a plan for success. Knowing your core five priorities will help you decide what to focus on and help drive all of the action in your business. When you build your business using the core five, you will stop taking meaningless action that doesn't get you anywhere.

Now that we have established the five pillars of a solid foundation, it's time to take a fresh look at some of the daily activities you are familiar with and some new activities you may want to adopt while completing your daily income-producing activities:

- Connect
- Invite
- Follow-up
- Collect a Decision
- Train

You should power these with tools that are simple and effective. It doesn't matter how you do these activities. You can do them in person, online, through paid funnels, or organically. Remember that network marketing has been around much longer than social media. We know that the methods may change slightly but the principles are solid.

There will always be the newest platform, but the activities stay the same. For example, you can create pique interest videos that are five minutes or less, simple to navigate websites, company-approved messaging, and apps for sharing and communication are expected and necessary for successful duplication and retention. New technologies force leaders and organizations to implement new and emerging platforms and techniques at a record pace which can create disruption and slow progress if systems aren't in place to keep everything stable through change.

Some people might feel they have a license to improve what they were given, and pretty quickly, the message is no longer compliant or effective, and no one knows who changed it. Every time this happens, your duplication system breaks. Remember the game "Telephone" that kids play? One person starts with a phrase and whispers it to the person next to them. That person then whispers what they *think* they heard to the next person, and on it goes. The last person then says out loud what they heard. Very rarely is it what the original person whispered.

This is what happens to systems when we all start tinkering around with them and tweaking them. The slightest shifts over time can change the message. A really great system that has worked in the past now doesn't have the same impact. So how do you know if your team is getting the same system? How do you even know if you have a system? It's three simple things:

1. Everyone knows the system

2. Everyone follows the system

3. The system works

This is key for success in your team. Take something like an invite and ask yourself if the newest person on your team knows it, follows it, and it works for them. If the answer is "no," then you need to go back to your system and figure out where the breakdown is.

Coach's Notes:

The great part about what Sue is teaching you is that not only does it **work** *very well, but anyone can implement these steps. Anyone can take these steps and then apply their own uniqueness and style. Sue has given you the foundation.*

The tools to build a business

When I started network marketing, it was different. Let's take a minute to compare that cassette tape I started with years ago to the tools and systems of today. There are times I wish we could go back to the cassette tape. It was a time of simplicity. You decided to join a company, you purchased 100 cassette tapes for $25, and it was your job to get those tapes in the hands of 100 people to listen to the message as quickly as possible. Next, you followed up and started those who joined you in the business the same way. Duplicating the purchase and placement of cassette tapes was the only system, everyone used it and it worked.

Full disclosure, after listening to the cassette tape message, we invited our prospects to a conference call to hear from a leader who shared the vision and a testimonial and an invitation to a hotel meeting when available. To accomplish this, you had to purchase supplies to mail the cassettes, photocopy material at a copy shop since there were no home copy machines, trips to the post office and postage, long-distance phone bills for calls with anyone outside of your city.

Enough of the trip down memory lane - you get the point. In all honesty, though, it really was simple compared to today. Today you can change every message with the swipe of a keystroke or a video edit. With the click of a button, you can now deliver your message instantly and without delivery cost. No longer are we seeing thousand-dollar phone bills as we enjoy flat rates or no long-distance charges along with free international communication access through apps like WhatsApp and Messenger.

Zoom allows a leader to facilitate a meeting for pennies or even free with guests attending free of charge from the comfort of their home or phone. Technology is the secret that has moved our businesses from home-based to phone-based and allowed more people than ever to obtain results using the cracks of their life that used to be wasted.

So, what are some secrets that work, and you've never heard about before? Some things can make building a business a little more fun and enjoyable. The secret to successfully implementing new activities and habits is to make your brain release dopamine and create fun ways to challenge yourself and complete things quickly. Another secret is that you have to develop habits by doing the action steps every day. Starting and stopping keep you at day one over and over again. You don't have to work all day every day, but you do have to do something each day to create the pattern and habit before you start skipping days. It only takes most people thirty days to fully develop a habit, and you can adjust your activities for your lifestyle to include family and faith one day each week. This is the game-changer.

One of my favorite things to do is our daily P's. Here is what you do. Start your day off with five minutes of inspiration. We have a Facebook group where the leaders post a five-minute video for the team to watch each day. We even use themes around P.O.W.E.R. Monday is Planned Productivity, Tuesday is Overcoming Objections, Wednesday is World Class, Thursday is Energized Engagement, and Friday is Radical Results.

Next is completing one or more power hours each day. Power hours are broken down into 15-minute sections with countdown clocks that help people stay on purpose and improve their skills to complete their activities faster. We offer some live power hours and provide a power hour webinar available 24/7 where they can meet individually or with a group at a time that fits their schedule and duplicates consistency.

The final daily P is to put on your PJ's every night. This is the most powerful activity of the day. Just before you are going to go to sleep, you Plan, Journal, then sleep. This simple step engages the subconscious mind to partner in your success. I want to break this down for you to understand your PJ's power. Always plan your day the night before. Look at your calendar and know what your plan is. Your subconscious is activated by decision, and when you make your plan, you are making a decision that activates your army of subconscious partners to work while you sleep. Journal for five minutes about how your day went. What worked and where did you struggle, what did you learn, and what you will do tomorrow are a few of the things that will just dump out of your brain each day. This makes space for new things tomorrow and will create a pattern of productivity and peace. Completing these two things before sleep will set you up for success and allow for better sleep as well.

Equation to success

Another unique piece of our system is truly monitoring your personal power of five, which works like this. We created a worksheet for each person's highest-producing sponsorship lines. It's an equation we call $4 + 1 + 1 + 1$ until. Remember that 80 percent of your income will come from your top three to five partners. Never will it be your first four. It will always be your best four. Find your first four quickly, then continue to sponsor and work your plan until you obtain the rank and income you want and help them obtain theirs. The real secret here is that if you follow this path, you will surpass each goal you set while cheering on your team to achieve theirs.

Just remember that the power of a system is your personal superpower. Every area of life that functions on systems becomes scalable and increases bottom line profits. Look at an airline, a franchise, a family, and even a freeway. They all function because of a system of processes and rules. They are always in the process of improvement or construction as well. Your success is dependent on you being hungry for a better life, being coachable by those who have achieved success already, and being willing to take action. Those who try to create their own road always get stuck, lost or simply stop.

I am grateful for my journey and the struggles that led me to the castle. I am grateful for the princess that was able to transform because of the opportunity that Network Marketing provided a girl who literally did not have a bedroom when she grew up. I really did sleep in a hide-a-bed in an unfinished basement. My parents loved me and wanted more for me as they did their best to navigate life.

The opportunity to move to the castle is real. The steps and inspiration of this group of authors is in your hands. Life doesn't change overnight but it does change over time if you commit to the journey and help others along the way. There has never been a greater need for families to find hope and a better life than right now in your family and in your neighborhood. It isn't just an opportunity; it is our responsibility!

I want to close my chapter with a challenge to trust your leaders, your company, and the system enough to plug in and go to work. You deserve everything that this industry and your company have to offer. The future is in your daily decisions, and we are excited for you to have your own Cinderella story.

Coach's Notes:

*The best system in the world doesn't work unless you work. Sue said at the very end something that is important to say again: "The future is in your **daily** decisions." The best system in the world doesn't make the business easy, but it does make it possible. It gives you clarity, focus, and leverage. So, follow the system and focus on getting a little better every day!*

TOCARRA JOHNSON

Achievements:

- Toccara Johnson has been in network marketing for five years
- She has been with her current company for one and a half years
- She is in the top 1 percent of her company
- Reached the top rank in her company in eight months
- Single mom of an eight-year-old daughter

Quote:
"Happiness cannot be traveled to, owned, earned, worn, or consumed. Happiness is the spiritual experience of living every minute with love, grace, and gratitude."

- Denis Waitley

Coach's Notes:

"Be you because everyone else is already taken." - Anonymous.

*It is nearly impossible to have true success until you **find yourself**! It is empowering to see so many people walk across the stage at a convention with different accolades. It is also discouraging for others to see this. We are a society of comparison. If you are going to compare, I say only do it in a way that uplifts you and your perspective. Is the glass half-full or half-empty? It is always full with a combo of air and water! Tocarra is another leader with contagious energy. I am telling you that having that energy is a theme! I didn't naturally have it like Tocarra. I had to learn to develop it. Let's discover how you can be your authentic self!*

Keys to success

One of the most important keys to being successful in network marketing is being authentically you. People spend so much time struggling to "find their voice." They say they don't know what to share on social media and how to show up. Why is this? When we can remember that the best thing we can do is be ourselves, it helps us connect and helps free us from having to be anyone but ourselves.

When people start network marketing, they usually have a mentor or upline that is helping them learn the business. Unfortunately, I see many people thinking they need to be exactly like their mentor. You do not need to be like your mentor, the top person in the company, or the biggest influencer. You get to be you. Learn from others, but then learn how to show up and use their tools and skills as yourself. When you authentically like yourself, you shine through when you are yourself and showing people what you love.

Maybe you are stuck getting back to knowing yourself. You just need to tap back into yourself. So here are a couple of questions to ask yourself. Think of this exercise as getting to know *Me*.

- What are things that I love right now?

- What did I love when I was younger?

- What are things that I can share with the world?

- What excites me? What do I spend my time getting excited about?

- What do I like to share with others?

- What are things important to me right now?

- What are some of my struggles? What do I see as an obstacle for me?

- What is something special about me?

Now I want you to think about yourself. How do you describe yourself to others when they ask you to tell them about you? Are you a mom? Where do you live? What do you do with your time? What hobbies do you love? What do you like? What is something fascinating about you? What are your passions? What are the top three things that inspired you in the past month?

As you read through these questions, I want you to check in with yourself. Are you answering the questions, or are you telling yourself you don't know the answer? You are the only one who can answer these! Make sure you take the time to get to know yourself. This is so important because when you can answer these questions, these are the things that will connect you with other people. I guarantee you there are many people out there in the world who also can relate to your exact things.

So why does getting to know yourself help your network marketing business? Let me give you an example of myself. I am a mother. I love cooking. I am also a person who likes to shop and find amazing deals. As you read these things about me, how many of these things helped connect you to me? Maybe one, maybe all!

Often, my audience enjoys that because women who are relatable to my age or mothers can relate to those same things. I guarantee you, your audience can relate to something that you love. It will help them get to know you and help you create some type of bond that will attract them to you.

You want to be relatable. I see people get on social media, and they try to edit themselves. They keep their posts curated to photoshoots and quotes. No one can get to know the true you if you aren't opening up and being yourself. Being relatable helps people see themselves in you. You have to be able to show and allow people to see themselves in you.

For example, I'm a mom. I could hide this part of my life and edit it out of my social media. But if I were to do this, I would be missing an opportunity to connect because I am not connecting with other people. When I share authentically about being a mom, another mom will link up to my story and post. I am also able to connect with my local community. As I share authentically, I am linked to things going on with myself as a mom and with my daughter. Another mom is going to connect through the things that are happening with her and her children. Most moms can relate.

When someone can see themselves in you, it creates a start to a relationship or a continued relationship because you are authentically you, and people want to see more of that. So, when they start falling in love with you, you will start connecting with more people and build a following of people who want to connect with you on social media and will begin to convert to people wishing to do business with you.

Authenticity doesn't mean you are perfect

When you are authentically yourself, perfection is not the goal. You don't have to be perfect. You don't have to show up and be the most perfect person in the world. People want to see the real you. That's what makes you relatable.

On top of that, when they see the real you, they see your life and what it looks like to *really* build a business. They see what the business is all about. I have heard people say that they don't want to "scare people away" from doing network marketing by authentically sharing the business. I have found the exact opposite to be true. The more I share, and the more I share authentically, the more I get people that are interested and reaching out to learn more. It helps people see that building a successful business is obtainable for them, and it won't always look perfect.

Be your imperfect, perfect self. Show people how you do calls with laundry in the background. Show people when you fail and how you balance work and family life. And make sure you are just perfectly imperfect. Perfectly imperfect is what people relate to. More people can relate to the blunders, mix-ups, and chaos than they can to the perfection that we all think is real life. Often, when something is perfect, people believe that it's not obtainable, and it's hard, and you're not going to attract the right people.

Showing people your authentic self isn't as easy as we think it will be. There is a huge key to being yourself. One important thing is being vulnerable, and this includes sharing about your journey. Tell some of the things that you have experienced. You don't have to share everything! But decide what you are willing to share and understand that it may be vulnerable for you to share. Our life experiences can be painful, messy, and raw - it is never perfect. But this is a part of our journey. Other people have that too. We want to share this part as well because it is what got us to where we are today. Guess what? A lot of people are going to relate to that.

A lot of people are going to want to say you know you. What you've been through, even if it is painful, could be the same thing that people can say, "Yes, I get it. I understand her." If your audience can see themselves in you and see that you can do it, they will start to think that they can do it as well. Being authentic, in your real self, being vulnerable, and pouring your heart out makes you relatable. There is no painting the perfect picture for our lives. There are just our messy, beautiful lives that we are all building. When you can show this, it builds trust. It builds trust in you.

Authenticity makes people build and buy

As people get to know more about you, even if they have never met you in person, they will start to connect to you. Have you ever been watching a movie and felt like you are best friends with the characters? This is because the connection isn't created by being with someone. Connection is created by what we are thinking. As you authentically post and share yourself, your life, and your business with people, they will start to connect to you. People are going to know more about you, even though they don't physically know you.

It helps to build up that relationship because now they're learning more about you. They see who you are. They see more about your life and can relate to some of the things you are interested in and posting. They will relate to something that you've experienced. All of this starts attracting people to you, and they are not only going to support your business, but they also may even be willing to join you in this business.

One way to connect with people online is that it doesn't always have to be about the business. You can also share free value. If you love to cook, show people how to make your favorite family recipe. If you love to do crafts, give people a list of your favorite resources. As you are sharing free value, people are starting to trust you to be a fun resource that they want to continually check-in and see what you are up to and what you are sharing. This continues to build trust and allows people to see who you authentically are.

Let your light shine. Walk into your true authentic self. Not only is it going to help you grow your business, but it's also going to help you attract a fantastic audience and create those relationships with your customers. This can eventually turn into business partnerships that will turn into excellent networking opportunities. As you share as your authentic self, they feel like they can relate to you. Your audience will feel like they know something about you. You create that trust.

Being authentic hasn't always come naturally to me. I found it hard to let people get to know me. I had to change how I was thinking about it. I had to see that if I could walk in my truth, that would inspire people. I learned that no matter what I was going through, other people would really connect if I could be authentic to my life. It became important to me to show people how to be themselves and teach them how to shine. I wanted people to know that they can do big things in life and business no matter what they are going through.

I am a single mom. It is hard being a single mom, but guess what? As I have shared my struggles and joys being a single mom, I have found my own light shining brighter. As I shine my light, people are attracted to my light. And the best part is that those people learn to turn their light on and shine it for themselves.

Coach's Notes:

A few of the headlines alone in this chapter should make you think.

"Authenticity makes people build and buy."

"Authenticity doesn't mean you are perfect."

*You will connect with many more people when you can come to grips that it is okay not to be perfect. Tocarra is constantly showing up as her authentic self. She connects so quickly with people who have never met her because she is willing to **show** who she really is - the good and the bad - the sad and the funny. And the whole irony of it is this: whatever struggle you think you have that is preventing you from more sales may be the message that will get you more sales!*

TYRONICA CARTER

- Native Mississippian now residing in GA with her husband and two sons
- Began network marketing in 2015
- Educator for fifteen years who was able to retire herself and her husband by the age of forty after only two years in the business
- Leads a team of over 119,000 consultants
- Holds second highest rank in the company
- 6 Figure Earner Award for four years in a row
- In 2020 received the 7 Figure Earner Award
- In 2020 was the GoPro Million Dollar Inductee
- In 2021 was the Women in Business Million Dollar Earner Honoree
- Personally earned over $5M in sales and team building in six years
- In 2020 total team sales exceeded $270,000,000
- She is the leader of Team Radiant Styles, where her slogan is "Outdream Yourself."
- Her goal now is to continue to provide the necessary tools to her team to see them all reach their goals and dreams, as she has

Quote:

"Once you see results, it becomes an addiction."

- Unknown

Coach's Notes:

*As you are reading this chapter and the rest of this book, stop to think about this. You have six and seven-figure earners sharing their best insights and secrets to help **you**! No, that doesn't make it easy, but it definitely makes it **easier**. You can learn from your own mistakes, or you can learn from others' mistakes. Tyronica is one of the few million-dollar **annual** earners. She is about to drop her top ten learning lessons. As Jim Rohn says, "Success leaves clues."*

10 things I've learned in six years of network marketing

I was an elementary school teacher for fifteen years—no background in business, no background in marketing, no background in entrepreneurship. I took a bold step to try something new, and boy, am I glad I did. Network marketing has changed my life. These past six years have been one roller coaster ride of highs, lows, successes, disappointments, failures, determination, and slowly transforming into someone I never knew I could be.

Now, being in the top eight of my entire company, I have reflected on some of the key things I believe have gotten me to the top, and I think they will help you too. If I could go back and tell my past self about the keys to having success in network marketing, these are the ten things I would tell my past self. You are on your way to success in this business. Use my experience and keys to success to get ahead in this business.

1. I determine my success.

Not one person, not one thing, no timetable, determines success. You determine how successful you are. Most of the successful people I know hit the ground running on day one! It's nice to have a supportive and present upline, but it's not always necessary for *your* success! It's not their fault, the company's fault, or your downline's fault that you are where you are. If you do not feel you are getting what you need to succeed, what will *you* do about changing that?

As I tell my team, turn that finger around and point it back at you! The team isn't producing or is falling off no matter how much you pour into them. They keep recruiting and building your team. You will sift through hundreds or even thousands before you actually have those that will stick and stay. So, keep sifting! You should always be a problem solver for your business. Always take actionable steps to ensure you see your success, and always make sure you are in the driver's seat.

2. *Find what works for* **you** *and* **master it!**

Frequently we try to tackle our business one way because we see someone else killing it in that manner. With so many tools and options available, you can find more suitable ways to who *you* are. What works for you will be different depending on your lifestyle and how you want to work. You have to find what works and then go all in making it work for you.

I hear people say that they just don't love jumping on social media, and then they blame that for why they aren't succeeding in the business. Not wanting or liking to go live is *not* the reason your business is failing. Remember, network marketing was around way before the ease of social media. As I often say, there's more than one way to skin a cat! If you're more of a people person, grab those events, create your own event, go back to doing home parties! If you're great with social media, be sure you are utilizing multiple social media outlets. Find the way that you are most comfortable with and master It! Become known for it! That doesn't mean it should be your only method of working your business, but have that one thing that you are known for and absolutely kill the game in!

If you continue to think that someone else has the key to your success, you will get stuck chasing other people's success and not finding your own. Once you find what works, master it.

> **Coach's Notes:**
>
> *Big insight! We confuse principles with techniques. What does this mean? When we hear the exact way a leader has success, we think we need to do it that exact way for duplication purposes. The goal should be deeper than that. Extract the principle. For example, my mentor had the dumbest approach (in my mind) of all time. He would call someone (this was fifteen years ago) and say, give me your credit card, and we will make a ton of money. Are you kidding me? I would never say that. So instead of applying the technique and repeating what he said word for word, I dug deeper. The principle was that the world loves boldness. The principle was how brief and bold he was. Now that I understood the principle, I could apply it with my own style and personality.*

3. Implement what you've learned in your season.

Sometimes the information thrown at us, whether you're just getting started, or are a veteran, can be very overwhelming. Trying to implement it all at once can discourage us or make us feel like you've taken on more than you can handle. That eventually leads to quitting or becoming very mediocre. I like to encourage my team to attend every meeting offered, take notes, and listen. *But* use the information given where you are in your business. Save the rest of the information for when you are in that season of your business.

Think about it. If you're in first grade, you must learn and master first-grade work to move on to the second, before you get to twelfth grade! I can listen to and watch how that twelfth-grade student works and executes, but if I'm not even close to their level of knowledge and skill, I shouldn't try to do what they do until I have mastered where I am. Know what season you are in and implement the skills for that season.

4. *Keep your blinders up!*

Comparison is the thief of joy! Learn to celebrate any and all of your wins, no matter how big or small you may think they are. It's a step forward. Of course, people will pass you and do things their way. But, you should always be yourself and use your talents to speak to your audience and following. It is absolutely okay to be happy for the next person's success, but don't take the focus off your goals and plans.

Don't become a spectator in a race you are supposed to be running! Don't fool yourself with the "My race, my pace" saying because that's not the case if you're only watching from the sideline, not even in the race! Instead, stay focused on what *you* came to do! Then, go back and use tips two and three to remind yourself what you have to do to stay in the race in this season of your business.

5. *Set a why and crush it to create a new why.*

We all know that we should have a "why" to continue being motivated and inspired to work our business. But did you know that the ultimate goal is to have an evolving why? Not because you've changed it because you find it difficult to reach, but because you are reaching it.

Your why should be continuously changing because as you work hard in your business and achieve new milestones, that should include achieving your *why*. For example, when I first began my business, my reason as an educator was to make an extra $500 a month. Little did I know I would reach that goal pretty fast because I loved what I did. I constantly shared my journey with my followers and stayed relevant. The love of my business was a huge inspiration and attraction. Within a month, not only did I reach that $500 goal, but my team had also grown, and I began my first climb in ranks with my company. This inspired me to create a new *why* and work hard to keep checking it off my list and growing.

6.   Be an inspiration to your team.

One of the best pieces of advice I received from someone when I first started the business was that "You can't motivate your team. You can only inspire them." I have lived by these words since early on in network marketing.

Your job as a leader is to inspire your team to be their best and work their business. You should be leading by example. You want them to be top sellers, be a top seller yourself, or at least show them you are doing what it takes to be one. You want them to be recruiting machines, then show them how you show up every day for your business and attract others through your influence. The inspiration they get from seeing you grow and work hard will intrinsically motivate them not to give up and keep going.

7.   It's ok to reinvent yourself and try new things as time evolves.

When I first started my business in 2015, Facebook Live did not exist. My team and I did things like home parties, online parties, vending events, etc. But in 2017, the game changed with Facebook Live! It boosted so many people's businesses and gave tons of exposure! I had to learn the game! We still do all of the previous ways listed above, but we realized it's okay to try new things and change with time. As we love to say, *Try Everything*! It is okay to upgrade your logo, customize your URL, or totally change up what isn't working. Sometimes we block our own growth in our business by refusing to move on to newer, bigger, and better ways of doing things.

As time evolves, technology and how we do business evolves. But here is what I want you to know. *You* will evolve too. So often, the biggest obstacle that people face is judgment from other people. As we start to do this business, we change. We begin to put ourselves out there and do more personal development. We are literally evolving by all the new concepts we learn and the new experiences we have. Don't get stuck because your friends and family are uncomfortable with your evolution. I have seen a picture that has a caterpillar talking to a butterfly, saying, "You have changed." The butterfly replies, "We are supposed to." We are made to evolve!

8. *Try something a million and one times before you decide it doesn't work.*

Listen, I know the definition of insanity is doing the same thing repeatedly and expecting a different result. Still, some of us come nowhere near close to being insane for your business! We are so quick to try it a week, a month, three months and write it off as not working when the truth is *you* didn't work it. Ouch! Consistency and reinvention are the key elements to success! So, as I tell my team, #DontGetOffTheRide! Stick it out and see it through.

People quit *way* too soon. I saw this in the education field, and I see it in network marketing all the time. Most often, people are quitting a process because they do not believe that it will work. Check your belief whenever you are frustrated and fed up. Instead of thinking it will never work, try shifting your belief to something like, "I wonder how this will work" or "I will keep at this and learn." That shift right there can help you stick with it and figure it out.

9. *Sales are the heart of the business.*

For most network marketing companies, sales are the heart of the business. Everything you want to achieve from recruiting, growing your customer base and followers, seeing an increase in sales, and seeing your team all do the same boils down to ensuring you are selling and being a product of the product.

We love to love people, make new connections, find great products to use, and become leaders. These are all fantastic things about the industry, but don't forget what the heart of the business is. When you lose heart, you die. The best example of this is the movie *Moana*. Te Fiti dies when she loses her heart. It isn't until Moana restores it that she flourishes once again. Sounds simple, but I have seen it happen time and time again in network marketing. People lose their heart, the focus on sales, and their business starts to die. They have two choices: they can die off *or* restore their heart and flourish once again. Life always offers us second chances.

10. Building and selling should have equal efforts to see real results.

For the most part, people do okay with their sales. With consistency, you will usually see results and growth. It's the recruiting we *think* we are terrible at and can't do. Well, to be honest, that's not the case. Think about it; you show your lives, post about the new products and incentives available, and sell to all of your friends and family. *But* do you put those same efforts consistently into your recruiting tactics? Are you sharing the opportunity often? Do you share your journey in the business of how much it's changed your life?

If I took a look at your social media page, would I only want to be your customer, or would the things you share also make me want to know more about what you do? To see the actual results of wealth and growth in your business, selling and recruiting should hold equal value. Therefore, 100 percent of your efforts should go toward selling, and 100 percent of your efforts should intentionally go towards recruiting.

We can all fail our way to success

As a former educator, I went almost blindly into network marketing. I did what I thought felt right and learned as I failed forward. My favorite quote is, "Once you see results, it becomes an addiction." I became addicted to the results I produced, especially the small ones. My only objective was to beat *my* best! Like I stated, my best doesn't come without failure. As you grow through network marketing, you will come up with your own life lessons that you learn.

My journey of success hasn't come by going from huge success to huge success. It came from small actions, small failures, and consistency. This industry has some of the most successful people in the world involved. There are thousands of millionaires in our industry, and every single one of them failed their way to success. You can do this. You can create a life you love to live.

You can create a lifestyle for your family that you only imagined in your wildest dreams. Success is already there. But you must be willing to fail your way to your desired results. Write your chapters in this journey. No one has a success story or has completed a book without chapters of highs, lows, happiness, sadness, victories, and disappointments. You have to write the chapters before you have a story to tell! Keep writing! You're going to have an amazing story one day!

Coach's Notes:

Start with ten things you have learned right now! Even if you haven't yet had success, I challenge you to start your list. You are creating your success story now. You are beginning to learn as much as you can. We now know that authentic learning means you are applying— your next challenge. Strive to find the principles in every training. That includes this book. Don't confuse the principles and techniques. This one skill will help propel your business big time! You just heard from a million-dollar annual earner. She just willingly shared with **you** *her top ten learning lessons. Don't take them for granted!*

CONCLUSION

This is the third collaboration book that I have been able to co-write with brilliant authors in the network marketing industry—each time, I find myself taking notes and gaining insight. I can't wait to see the impact that this book and these people will continue to make. These books are read worldwide in every single nation. Now that you have this book, I want to encourage you to make an action plan. Go through it once more and create actionable steps that you are going to take in your business. Small steps lead to big results.

Knowledge is powerful, but only if you utilize it. We live in a world of consumption. Knowledge is no different. You can consume knowledge every single day, but what are you doing with it? That is the essential part. You can be the biggest "book expert" in your field, but you know nothing if you have never actually *played* in your field. Now, get out there and go and play.

If you want to find more ways to utilize these tools, mastermind with other top earners, or find a community of network marketers, check out my Facebook community or robsperry.com for other great resources. I have many great events coming up, and I don't want you to miss them.